LIBRARY USE OF THE MEGA INTERNET SITES, 2011-12 Edition

Google, Facebook, Yahoo!, Twitter, YouTube, Wikipedia, and More

ISBN 1-57440-177-7

Library of Congress Control Number: 2011936693

T OF TABLES

TABLE OF CONTENTS

THE QUESTIONNAIRE

LIBRARY SIZE CHARACTERISTICS

1. What is the annual budget for all purposes, including salaries, materials, building maintenance, etc.?

COLLECTION DIGITIZATION

2. Is the library currently working with any search engine or other organization to digitize elements of its collection and make this element available over the internet?

3. If the library is not currently working with any search engine or other organization to digitize elements of its collection and make that element available over the internet, what is the likelihood that you will follow such a course over the next two years?

MEGA INTERNET SITES IN INFORMATION LITERACY WORKSHOPS

4. Has the library ever conducted workshops for patrons that include instruction in how to use any of the following?

    A.   Google Books
    B.   Google Maps
    C.   Google Scholar
    D.   Google Buzz
    E.   Yahoo Groups
    F.   Flickr
    G.   Tumblr
    H.   LibraryThing
    I.   Yahoo Maps
    J.   Bing search engine
    K.   Google search engine
    L.   YouTube
    M.   LinkedIn
    N.   Facebook
    O.   Blogger.com
    P.   Twitter
    Q.   Wordpress.com

USEFULNESS OF VARIOUS INTERNET SITES

5. Rate the usefulness of the following sites in your professional library work:

    A.   Google Books
    B.   Google Maps

C. Google RealTime
D. Google Translate
E. Google Scholar
F. Google Buzz
G. Yahoo Groups
H. Flickr
I. Tumblr
J. LibraryThing
K. Yahoo Maps
L. Bing search engine
M. Google search engine
N. LinkedIn
O. YouTube
P. Wikipedia
Q. Blogger.com
R. Twitter
S. Wordpress.com

THE LIBRARY AND LIBRARYTHING

6. Which phrase best describes your understanding of and use of the internet site LibraryThing?

A. Don't really know what it is.
B. Have heard of it but we don't use it.
C. We use it a little.
D. We use it a lot.
E. We love it.

7. If your library uses LibraryThing, briefly describe how you use it and how the library benefits.

THE LIBRARY AND TWITTER

8. Does the library have a Twitter account?

9. How many tweets does your library send out in a typical or average month?

10. To the best of your knowledge how many subscribers does your library's Twitter account have?

SOCIAL NETWORKING SITES

11. Rate the usefulness of the following social networking sites to your work or the library in general:

A.   MySpace
B.   Facebook
C.   Bebo
D.   Friendster
E.   Ning
F.   Hi5
G.   Orkut
H.   MyLife
I.   Multiply

12. If it has a presence on the site, approximately how many unique visits does the library receive per month on average to the following sites?

    A.   MySpace
    B.   Facebook
    C.   Other sites

13. Has your library developed specific pages on Facebook or on other social networks for special collections or library departments?

USE OF AMAZON

14. Has the library ever purchased an e-book from Amazon or an e-book in conjunction with a print title?

15. How much has the library spent on Amazon in the past year to acquire traditional books, e-books or parts of books?

16. How much has the library spend on all other online booksellers in the past year to acquire traditional books, e-books or parts of books?

17. Does the library in any way take advantage of the Amazon web services program that allows libraries to use cover images, reviews, book descriptions and other book-related information from the Amazon site in the library OPAC or in other library contexts?

VIDEO & PHOTO SHARING

18. Does the library have one or more YouTube accounts?

19. Do you use any of the following in your professional library work?

    A.   AOL Video
    B.   Blip TV
    C.   Brightcove
    D.   DailyMotion

E.   Facebook
F.   Flickr Video
G.   GoFish
H.   Google Buzz
I.   Google Video
J.   Hulu
K.   MetaCafe
L.   Photobucket
M.   Revver
N.   Viddler
O.   Vimeo
P.   Vzaar
Q.   Yahoo Video
R.   Yfrog
S.   YouTube

20. How many visits did the library get to its YouTube site in the past year?

21. Has the library ever posted any photos of the library or library special events on Flickr (the Yahoo photo sharing site)?

22. Has the library ever posted any photos from the library collection on Flickr?

23. Has the library ever posted any photos taken by library patrons on Flickr?

24. Has the library ever used YouTube in training library patrons to use the library?

25. If the library has posted videos or photos about itself or its collections on internet photo and video sites, please mention a few of the most useful or prominent sites.

THE LIBRARY AND GOOGLE BOOKS

26. Which phrase best describes your library staff's use of Google Books?

   A.   We don't really use it.
   B.   We use it occasionally.
   C.   We use it extensively.

27. Which phrase best captures the library's plans for contributing content to Google Books?

   A.   We have already digitized part of our collection and contribute some of our non-copyright works to Google Books.
   B.   We have already digitized parts of our collection but have not contributed to Google Books.

C.   We have not digitized any part of our collection but plan to in the near future.

D.   We have not digitized any part of our collection and do not plan to in the near future.

SURVEY PARTICIPANTS

Albion College
American University
Anderson County Library
Andrew College
Arkansas State University-Mountain Home
Auburn Montgomery Library
Bellingham Public Library
Billy Graham Evangelistic Association
Brooklyn College
Bryan Cave LLP
Burlington Public Library
Butte College
California Court of Appeal, Third District
Carroll Community College
Cassels Brock & Blackwell LLP
Consortium Information Services, Inc.
Davenport University
Douglas County Libraries
Eckerd College
Edward Nathan Sonnensbergs Inc
Emporia State University- White Library
Eugene Public Library
Euless Public library
Fairport Public Library
FamilySearch
Farella Braun + Martel LLP
Florida Southern College
Flower Mound Public Library
Grand County Public Library
Greenfield Public Library
Hampton University
Hawley Troxell Ennis & Hawley LLP
Hiscock & Barclay LLP
HOK
Holland & Knight LLP
Homewood Public Library
IDC (Australia)
Ivins Phillips Barker
John Jay College
Kronick Moskovitz Tiedemann & Girard
LaFollette Public Library
Lewes Public Library
Lewis University

Loutit District Library
Loyola Marymount University
Lyon County Law Library
Mercer County Community College
Mid-Continent University
Missouri River Regional Library
Morris County Library
Naperville Public Library
Narberth Community Library
New Braunfels Public Library
New York State Small Business Development Center
Olathe Public Library
Olivet Nazarene University
Olney Public Library
Oswego Public Library
Palo Verde Library
Palomar Community College
Paramus Public Library
Peoria Public Library
Phillips Lytle LLP
Princeton University
Querrey & Harrow
Quincy Public Library
Randolph-Macon College
Sacramento Public Library
Saint Louis University
San Francisco Public Library
Sidley Austin LLP
South Berwick Public Library
Southeastern Community College
St. Cloud State University
St. Paul Public Library
Starke County Public Library
State Library of Louisiana
Strayer University
Supreme Court of Canada
Swarthmore College Peace Collection
Texas Tech University
The U.S. Army Field Band
Thompson Hine LLP
Tompkins County Public Library
U.S. Dept. of the Interior/BOEMRE
Union University
University of Baltimore
University of British Columbia
University of British Columbia Library

University of California, Davis
University of Connecticut
University of Houston
University of Idaho Library
University of Illinois at Urbana
University of Kansas
University of New Hampshire – Dimond Library
University of Rhode Island
University of Tennessee at Chattanooga
University of Wisconsin-Whitewater
US Air Force
Washington State University Libraries
Washington State University Vancouver
White Mountain Library
Williamson County Public Library
Ypsilanti District Library

SUMMARY OF MAIN FINDINGS

Collection Digitization

Only 29% of the libraries in the sample were currently working with search engines or other organizations to digitize elements of their collections and make them available over the internet. A significant portion of these were college libraries, 48% of which were working to this effect. Among library personnel, those working in administration and technical services/cataloging were less likely to be active in making their collections available online, while those working with special collections were more likely.

Relatively few libraries not currently making their collections available online were pursuing this option, with 84% of the sample claiming it was unlikely that that they would enter into discussions or sign an agreement to do so within the next two years. Personnel working in technical services/cataloging expressed a greater interest than those in other departments, 43% claiming they were likely to discuss partnering with search engines or other parties within the next two years, and 14% were already involved in these discussions.

Information Literacy Workshops & the Mega Internet Sites

The Google search engine was the most widely taught technology in workshops led by libraries in the sample, with 44% of libraries having included this kind of instruction. It was frequently taught in both public and private libraries and across all library personnel. Only 4% of the libraries in the sample included the Bing search engine in their workshops.

Instruction in social networking sites like Facebook and Twitter were most common in public libraries, though much less so in institutional and corporate libraries. 60% of public libraries in the sample have held workshops in Facebook use; only 17.39% of college libraries, 10.53% of law/corporate libraries, and 14.29% of government agency/department libraries have done so. Flickr was another technology commonly taught in workshops by public libraries, but less so in others.

Most libraries had never conducted workshops that included instruction in Google Books, Google Buzz, or Google Maps. Google Scholar was more popular, with 40% of libraries in the sample including it in their workshops, though none of these were public libraries. Instruction in some of these programs was popular with college and university libraries, 70% of which taught use of Google Scholar, and 32% Google Books.

7.48% of libraries had conducted workshops which included instruction in the use of Blogger.com. 8.41% had done so with Wordpress.com, including 15.22% of college and university libraries and 33.33% of those working in acquisitions and collection development. None of the libraries in the sample instructed patrons in the use of Tumblr.

Workshops in programs like Yahoo Groups, Yahoo Maps, YouTube, and the cataloging site Library Thing were infrequent, and LinkedIn was especially unpopular at college libraries, of which only 4.35% offered instruction in use of the site. 10.28% of all the libraries in the sample offered instruction in LinkedIn, including 15.79% of law/corporate libraries and 17.39% of libraries with budgets greater than $10,000,000.

Usefulness of Various Internet Sites

72% of libraries in the sample reported that the Google Search Engine was highly useful, and only 3% did not use it at all. LinkedIn was popular among law/corporate libraries and government libraries, 26% and 29% finding it highly useful, though 42% of college libraries said it was not very useful, and 27% of those same libraries did not use it at all.

Google Books was found useful by 21.90% and highly useful by 16.19% of the sample. Another 35.24% of libraries found it occasionally useful. College and university libraries found it more useful than others, with 22.22% rating it highly useful and only 2.22% not very useful, though 8.89% did not use it or know of it. Google Maps was slightly better known and was considered useful or highly useful by 52.88% of libraries. Public libraries were its biggest fans, 91.18% of which found it useful to some extent. Comparatively, Yahoo Maps was considered useful or highly useful by only 20.39% of the sample, and was unknown by 33.98%.

76.7% of libraries in the sample did not use or know of Google RealTime, while Google Translate was rated occasionally useful by 38.83% and useful or highly useful by another 25.24%. Google Scholar was considered highly useful by 29.25% of the sample, and performed better among college/university libraries and law/corporate libraries, 41.3% and 42.11% of which rated it highly useful. Public libraries did not feel the same way, 29.41% of which did not use it, and an additional 11.76% of which found it not very useful.

Only 7.92% of libraries found Google Buzz at all helpful, and 71.29% did not use it or know of it. Yahoo Groups was not used by 45.10% of libraries, and of those that used it, 9.8% found it useful and none highly useful. Flickr was not considered very useful to professional library work by 25.47% of libraries and 26.42% did not use it at all.

None of the libraries in the sample found Tumblr highly useful and as many as 65.05% of them did not use it. LibraryThing performed slightly better, though 26.26% of the sample considered it not very useful, and nearly 40% had not used it or did not know of it. The Bing Search Engine was found occasionally useful by 27.88%, but 51.92% of libraries did not find it useful or did not use it. My Space was not used by 50.96% of libraries, and less than 1% found it useful or highly useful.

YouTube was rated highly useful by 16.04% of libraries, and another 63.21% rated it useful or occasionally useful. Only 9.43% of libraries did not use or know of YouTube, and this percentage is smaller among public libraries. Facebook was also considered useful to some degree by most libraries, 17.92% of which found it highly useful, and 31.43% of public libraries found it highly useful.

40.95% of libraries found Wikipedia useful, and another 25.71% found it highly useful. Those working in technical services and cataloging found it especially useful, 71.43% of these workers rating it highly useful, and the remaining 28.57% useful. Wikipedia was rated least useful by law and corporate libraries, 15.795 of which considered it not very useful and 10.53% of which did not use it.

Approximately 37% of the sample reported that they did not use or know of Wordpress or Blogger.com. Though 42.86% of public libraries did not use Blogger.com, 28.58% of the sample rated it useful or highly useful. 66.67% of personnel in special collections departments did not use Blogger.com, while the same percentage of those working in acquisitions and collection development considered it occasionally useful. Only 3.03% pf public libraries found Wordpress.com highly useful, and 18.18% of public libraries considered it not very useful. College and university libraries responded more positively, with 11.11% rating it highly useful and an additional 17.78% useful. Wordpress was also most popular with the acquisitions and collection development department, 33.33% of which considered it highly useful.

Twitter was rated highly useful by 12.26% of libraries, though less so in college and university libraries, 28.89% of which found it not very useful. 30.19% of all the libraries in the sample did not use Twitter, and as many as 71.43% of workers in technical services and cataloging and 50% of those working in special collections. Libraries with budgets greater than $10,000,000 used it more than those with smaller budgets, 26.09% of these rating it useful and 13.04% highly useful.

The Library and LibraryThing

61% of libraries in the sample reported that they knew of LibraryThing, but did not use it. Another 16% had not heard of it, and 13% used it a little. LibraryThing does seem to have a small group of enthusiastic users, with 11% of public libraries saying they love it and 15% of government libraries using it a lot.

The Library and Twitter

Almost 41% of libraries have a Twitter account. This includes 61% of public libraries, 40% of college libraries, and nearly 30% of government libraries, though less than 6% of law and corporate libraries have Twitter accounts...

The mean amount of tweets libraries send out per month is 32, with the maximum at 300 and the minimum at 0. On average, the libraries in the sample had 416 subscribers and some public libraries had as many as 2500.

Use of Social Networking Sites

While most libraries did not find social networking sites especially useful, Facebook was an exception to this rule. 21.7% of libraries considered Facebook very useful, and another 47.55% useful or somewhat useful. In contrast, 86.67% said that MySpace was not very useful, only 12.38% considered it somewhat useful and less than 1% considered it very useful or useful.

Only 2% of libraries found Bebo useful or somewhat useful. 1% of libraries found Friendster useful to some degree, and all of these were college and university libraries. Only 6.6% of libraries found Ning useful or somewhat useful. None of the libraries in the sample found Hi5 or Orkut at all useful. Approximately 1% found Multiply and MyLife useful to some degree, and these were limited to college and university libraries.

The libraries that maintained an online presence on Facebook received a mean of 971.66 unique visits to their Facebook page per month, with the minimum visits at 3 and the maximum at 12,000 visits per month. None of the libraries reported any visits to their MySpace page.

Additionally, 35.29% of libraries in the sample used pages on Facebook or other social networks for specific collections or library departments. These included 39.39% of public libraries and 44.44% of college and university libraries.

Use of Amazon

35.71% of libraries had at one time purchased e-books from Amazon or in conjunction with print titles, including 52.38% of college and university libraries, and 36.84% of law and corporate libraries in the sample. This trend was less pronounced in public libraries, only 19.35% of which had made such purchases, and in government agency and department libraries where none had.

Libraries spent a mean of $6,823.40 on traditional book and e-book purchases from Amazon in the last year, some spending as much as $150,000. College and university libraries spent the most on purchases from Amazon, with a mean of $14,491.18, and public libraries were a distant second, with a mean of $2,144.20 per year.

The libraries in the sample spent more on purchases from online booksellers other than Amazon, with a mean of $15,222.97, and the maximum amount spent on these purchases by single library was $100,000. College and university libraries still led the pack, spending a mean of $19,808.33 on such purchases, and a minimum of $200. Research and subject specialists accounted for the largest individual share of this spending, with a mean of $38,000, as opposed to a mean of $5,566.67 on Amazon purchases by the same group.

25% of libraries sold digital or print on demand copies of digitized works which copyrights had expired or for which they were given copyright permission. These sales were all attributed to college and university libraries and were further limited to those working in reference and information literacy.

37.89% of libraries did not and had no plans to use the Amazon web services program which allows libraries to use cover images, reviews, descriptions, and other book-related information from the Amazon site for their public catalogues or other library use. Another 18.95% of libraries had never heard of this program, while 22.11% had somewhat taken advantage of it, and 8.42% used it extensively. None of the law/corporate or government agency/department libraries in the sample were currently using this program.

Video & Photo Sharing Sites

36.63% of libraries maintained one or more YouTube accounts, and 5.94% planned to sign up for a YouTube account within the next year. These percentages increased to 51.22% and 9.09% in public libraries, and to 42.22% and 4.44% in college and university libraries, but were much smaller in the case of corporate and government libraries.

Other video and photo sharing services were less popular. Only 1.03% of libraries used AOL Video for professional library work, while 4.12% used Blip TV, all of these public libraries. 98.96% of libraries did not use Brightcove and 98.95% did not use DailyMotion.

73% of libraries used Facebook to post video, the largest concentration in public libraries, 81.82% of which used the service. Facebook was widely used by all the libraries in the sample and in every department. Flickr Video was used by 18.56% of libraries, least of which in law and corporate libraries, 94.44% of which reported no usage.

6.06% of the libraries in the sample used GoFish for video sharing. 17% used Google Video and 17.53% used Hulu in their professional work. Hulu was most popular among law and corporate libraries, of which 31.58% used the site.

MetaCafe was used by 2.08% of libraries, and only by administrative workers in public and college/university libraries. 11.11% of libraries used Photobucket to view or share videos and photographs, and none of the libraries in the sample used Revver or Viddler.

12.37% of the entire sample used Vimeo, 16.13% of public libraries, 7.14% of college and university libraries, and 21.05% of law/corporate libraries. 66.67% of personnel in acquisitions and collection development used Vimeo for their professional work.1.04% of libraries used Vzaar, 7.22% used Yahoo Video, and 3.06% used Yfrog, none of which were used by government agency and department libraries. Though few libraries used Yahoo Video, it was used by as many as 20% of special collections and 33.33% of acquisitions and collections development personnel.

Flickr was used by 34.58% of libraries to post photos of the library or of library special events. Fewer libraries posted photos from their collections on Flickr, 13.08%, and even fewer posted photographs taken by patrons, 6.98% of the sample.

In total, 63.27% of libraries used YouTube for professional work. It was used least by administration workers, 48.84%, but by 100% of workers in acquisitions and collection development. On average, library YouTube pages received 3,834 visits over the past year and as many as 30,800 visits. College and university libraries received the most visits, with a mean of 4597.08 in the last year.

34.78% of college and university libraries had at one time used YouTube to train library patrons to use the library, and 21.5% of all the libraries in the sample had done so. 42.87% of technical services and cataloging personnel used YouTube to teach patrons about library use, significantly more than their coworkers in other departments.

The Library and Google Books

While 38.28% of libraries reported that their staff does not use Google Books, 56.57% use it occasionally, and another 5.05% use it extensively. Nearly 80% of college and university libraries use Google Books occasionally or extensively, compared with 37.50% of public libraries. The service was used most extensively by research or subject specialists and those working in acquisitions and collection development, and 100% of those working in special collections said they use Google Books occasionally.

74.49% of libraries in the sample have not digitized any part of their collection and do not intend to in the near future. Another 3.06% plan to, but have not yet done so. 6.12% of libraries have digitized pieces of their collection and contributed some to Google Books, while a larger percentage, 16.33%, have also digitized works but are not contributing them to Google Books.

Libraries of colleges and universities have digitized parts of their collections more than others and 11.63% of college libraries are currently contributing digital works to Google Books. Only reference/information literacy and research/subject specialist personnel have contributed to Google Books, even as 40% of those in special collections and 28.57% of those in technical services and cataloging have already digitized parts of their collections. Libraries with budgets over $10,000,000 have digitized the most, and 26.32% have contributed portions of their collections to Google Books.

1. Library Size Characteristics

Table 1.1: What is the annual budget for all purposes, including salaries, materials, building maintenance, etc.?

	MEAN	MEDIAN	MINIMUM	MAXIMUM
Entire Sample	$6,243,981.71	$1,200,000.00	$50,000.00	$81,800,000.00

Table 1.2: What is the annual budget for all purposes, including salaries, materials, building maintenance, etc.? Broken out by type of library.

	MEAN	MEDIAN	MINIMUM	MAXIMUM
Public Library	$7,237,925.86	$1,938,462.00	$60,000.00	$81,800,000.00
College/University Library	$8,758,827.10	$1,500,000.00	$90,000.00	$35,000,000.00
Law/Corporate Library	$1,255,746.15	$500,000.00	$75,000.00	$5,000,000.00
Government Agency/Department Library	$258,333.33	$175,000.00	$50,000.00	$550,000.00

Table 1.3: What is the annual budget for all purposes, including salaries, materials, building maintenance, etc.? Broken out by professional position at the library.

	MEAN	MEDIAN	MINIMUM	MAXIMUM
Reference or Information Literacy	$7,193,194.12	$1,800,000.00	$90,000.00	$35,000,000.00
Research or Subject Specialist	$5,488,823.53	$500,000.00	$50,000.00	$20,000,000.00
Administration	$5,424,570.54	$1,000,000.00	$60,000.00	$81,800,000.00
Technical Services or Cataloging	$2,573,983.54	$1,200,000.00	$85,000.00	$17,606,786.00
Special Collections	$5,490,000.00	$1,700,000.00	$300,000.00	$15,000,000.00
Acquisitions or Collection Development	$17,051,800.00	$17,051,800.00	$1,000,000.00	$33,103,600.00

2. Collection Digitization

Table 2.1: Is the library currently working with any search engine or other organization to digitize elements of its collection and make this element available over the internet?

	YES	NO
Entire Sample	28.97%	71.03%

Table 2.2: Is the library currently working with any search engine or other organization to digitize elements of its collection and make this element available over the internet? Broken out by type of library.

	YES	NO
Public Library	14.29%	85.71%
College/University Library	47.83%	52.17%
Law/Corporate Library	15.79%	84.21%
Government Agency/Department Library	14.29%	85.71%

Table 2.3: Is the library currently working with any search engine or other organization to digitize elements of its collection and make this element available over the internet? Broken out by professional position at the library.

	YES	NO
Reference or Information Literacy	41.18%	58.82%
Research or Subject Specialist	46.15%	53.85%
Administration	11.36%	88.64%
Technical Services or Cataloging	14.29%	85.71%
Special Collections	60.00%	40.00%
Acquisitions or Collection Development	33.33%	66.67%

Table 2.4: Is the library currently working with any search engine or other organization to digitize elements of its collection and make this element available over the internet? Broken out by total library budget.

	YES	NO
Less than $1,000,000	21.05%	78.95%
Between $1,000,000 - $5,000,000	21.05%	78.95%
Between $5,000,000 - $10,000,000	25.00%	75.00%
Over $10,000,000	56.52%	43.48%

Table 2.5:   If the library is not currently working with any search engine or other organization to digitize elements of its collection and make that element available over the internet, what is the likelihood that you will follow such a course over the next two years?

	WE ARE ALREADY HAVING DISCUSSIONS WITH A SEARCH ENGINE OR OTHER PARTY	WE ARE LIKELY TO ENTER DISCUSSIONS OR ACTUALLY SIGN AN AGREEMENT WITHIN THE NEXT TWO YEARS	IT IS UNLIKELY THAT WE WILL ENTER DISCUSSIONS OR SIGN AN AGREEMENT OVER THE NEXT TWO YEARS
Entire Sample	5.06%	11.39%	83.54%

Table 2.6:   If the library is not currently working with any search engine or other organization to digitize elements of its collection and make that element available over the internet, what is the likelihood that you will follow such a course over the next two years? Broken out by type of library.

	WE ARE ALREADY HAVING DISCUSSIONS WITH A SEARCH ENGINE OR OTHER PARTY	WE ARE LIKELY TO ENTER DISCUSSIONS OR ACTUALLY SIGN AN AGREEMENT WITHIN THE NEXT TWO YEARS	IT IS UNLIKELY THAT WE WILL ENTER DISCUSSIONS OR SIGN AN AGREEMENT OVER THE NEXT TWO YEARS
Public Library	3.23%	6.45%	90.32%
College/University Library	4.00%	16.00%	80.00%
Law/Corporate Library	6.25%	18.75%	75.00%
Government Agency/Department Library	14.29%	0.00%	85.71%

Table 2.7: If the library is not currently working with any search engine or other organization to digitize elements of its collection and make that element available over the internet, what is the likelihood that you will follow such a course over the next two years? Broken out by professional position at the library.

	WE ARE ALREADY HAVING DISCUSSIONS WITH A SEARCH ENGINE OR OTHER PARTY	WE ARE LIKELY TO ENTER DISCUSSIONS OR ACTUALLY SIGN AN AGREEMENT WITHIN THE NEXT TWO YEARS	IT IS UNLIKELY THAT WE WILL ENTER DISCUSSIONS OR SIGN AN AGREEMENT OVER THE NEXT TWO YEARS
Reference or Information Literacy	0.00%	20.00%	80.00%
Research or Subject Specialist	12.50%	12.50%	75.00%
Administration	5.13%	2.56%	92.31%
Technical Services or Cataloging	14.29%	42.86%	42.86%
Special Collections	0.00%	0.00%	100.00%
Acquisitions or Collection Development	0.00%	0.00%	100.00%

Table 2.8: If the library is not currently working with any search engine or other organization to digitize elements of its collection and make that element available over the internet, what is the likelihood that you will follow such a course over the next two years? Broken out by total library budget.

	WE ARE ALREADY HAVING DISCUSSIONS WITH A SEARCH ENGINE OR OTHER PARTY	WE ARE LIKELY TO ENTER DISCUSSIONS OR ACTUALLY SIGN AN AGREEMENT WITHIN THE NEXT TWO YEARS	IT IS UNLIKELY THAT WE WILL ENTER DISCUSSIONS OR SIGN AN AGREEMENT OVER THE NEXT TWO YEARS
Less than $1,000,000	9.68%	3.23%	87.10%
Between $1,000,000 - $5,000,000	0.00%	18.75%	81.25%
Between $5,000,000 - $10,000,000	0.00%	0.00%	100.00%
Over $10,000,000	9.09%	18.18%	72.73%

3. Mega Internet Sites in Information Literacy Workshops

Table 3.1: Has the library ever conducted workshops for patrons that include instruction in how to use Google Books?

	YES	NO
Entire Sample	17.76%	82.24%

Table 3.2: Has the library ever conducted workshops for patrons that include instruction in how to use Google Books? Broken out by type of library.

	YES	NO
Public Library	0.00%	100.00%
College/University Library	32.61%	67.39%
Law/Corporate Library	15.79%	84.21%
Government Agency/Department Library	14.29%	85.71%

Table 3.3: Has the library ever conducted workshops for patrons that include instruction in how to use Google Books? Broken out by professional position at the library.

	YES	NO
Reference or Information Literacy	29.41%	70.59%
Research or Subject Specialist	23.08%	76.92%
Administration	6.82%	93.18%
Technical Services or Cataloging	14.29%	85.71%
Special Collections	20.00%	80.00%
Acquisitions or Collection Development	33.33%	66.67%

Table 3.4: Has the library ever conducted workshops for patrons that include instruction in how to use Google Books? Broken out by total library budget.

	YES	NO
Less than $1,000,000	18.42%	81.58%
Between $1,000,000 - $5,000,000	13.16%	86.84%
Between $5,000,000 - $10,000,000	0.00%	100.00%
Over $10,000,000	30.43%	69.57%

Table 3.5: Has the library ever conducted workshops for patrons that include instruction in how to use Google Maps?

	YES	NO
Entire Sample	13.08%	86.92%

Table 3.6: Has the library ever conducted workshops for patrons that include instruction in how to use Google Maps? Broken out by type of library.

	YES	NO
Public Library	2.86%	97.14%
College/University Library	23.91%	76.09%
Law/Corporate Library	10.53%	89.47%
Government Agency/Department Library	0.00%	100.00%

Table 3.7: Has the library ever conducted workshops for patrons that include instruction in how to use Google Maps? Broken out by professional position at the library.

	YES	NO
Reference or Information Literacy	20.59%	79.41%
Research or Subject Specialist	15.38%	84.62%
Administration	6.82%	93.18%
Technical Services or Cataloging	14.29%	85.71%
Special Collections	0.00%	100.00%
Acquisitions or Collection Development	33.33%	66.67%

Table 3.8: Has the library ever conducted workshops for patrons that include instruction in how to use Google Maps? Broken out by total library budget.

	YES	NO
Less than $1,000,000	10.53%	89.47%
Between $1,000,000 - $5,000,000	7.89%	92.11%
Between $5,000,000 - $10,000,000	12.50%	87.50%
Over $10,000,000	26.09%	73.91%

Table 3.9: Has the library ever conducted workshops for patrons that include instruction in how to use Google Scholar?

	YES	NO
Entire Sample	40.19%	59.81%

Table 3.10: Has the library ever conducted workshops for patrons that include instruction in how to use Google Scholar? Broken out by type of library.

	YES	NO
Public Library	0.00%	100.00%
College/University Library	69.57%	30.43%
Law/Corporate Library	42.11%	57.89%
Government Agency/Department Library	42.86%	57.14%

Table 3.11: Has the library ever conducted workshops for patrons that include instruction in how to use Google Scholar? Broken out by professional position at the library.

	YES	NO
Reference or Information Literacy	44.12%	55.88%
Research or Subject Specialist	69.23%	30.77%
Administration	27.27%	72.73%
Technical Services or Cataloging	28.57%	71.43%
Special Collections	60.00%	40.00%
Acquisitions or Collection Development	33.33%	66.67%

Table 3.12: Has the library ever conducted workshops for patrons that include instruction in how to use Google Scholar? Broken out by total library budget.

	YES	NO
Less than $1,000,000	39.47%	60.53%
Between $1,000,000 - $5,000,000	36.84%	63.16%
Between $5,000,000 - $10,000,000	25.00%	75.00%
Over $10,000,000	52.17%	47.83%

Table 3.13: Has the library ever conducted workshops for patrons that include instruction in how to use Google Buzz?

	YES	NO
Entire Sample	0.93%	99.07%

Table 3.14: Has the library ever conducted workshops for patrons that include instruction in how to use Google Buzz? Broken out by type of library.

	YES	NO
Public Library	0.00%	100.00%
College/University Library	2.17%	97.83%
Law/Corporate Library	0.00%	100.00%
Government Agency/Department Library	0.00%	100.00%

Table 3.15: Has the library ever conducted workshops for patrons that include instruction in how to use Google Buzz? Broken out by professional position at the library.

	YES	NO
Reference or Information Literacy	0.00%	100.00%
Research or Subject Specialist	0.00%	100.00%
Administration	0.00%	100.00%
Technical Services or Cataloging	0.00%	100.00%
Special Collections	0.00%	100.00%
Acquisitions or Collection Development	33.33%	66.67%

Table 3.16: Has the library ever conducted workshops for patrons that include instruction in how to use Google Buzz? Broken out by total library budget.

	YES	NO
Less than $1,000,000	0.00%	100.00%
Between $1,000,000 - $5,000,000	0.00%	100.00%
Between $5,000,000 - $10,000,000	0.00%	100.00%
Over $10,000,000	4.35%	95.65%

Table 3.17: Has the library ever conducted workshops for patrons that include instruction in how to use Yahoo Groups?

	YES	NO
Entire Sample	0.94%	99.06%

Table 3.18: Has the library ever conducted workshops for patrons that include instruction in how to use Yahoo Groups? Broken out by type of library.

	YES	NO
Public Library	0.00%	100.00%
College/University Library	2.22%	97.78%
Law/Corporate Library	0.00%	100.00%
Government Agency/Department Library	0.00%	100.00%

Table 3.19: Has the library ever conducted workshops for patrons that include instruction in how to use Yahoo Groups? Broken out by professional position at the library.

	YES	NO
Reference or Information Literacy	2.94%	97.06%
Research or Subject Specialist	0.00%	100.00%
Administration	0.00%	100.00%
Technical Services or Cataloging	0.00%	100.00%
Special Collections	0.00%	100.00%
Acquisitions or Collection Development	0.00%	100.00%

Table 3.20: Has the library ever conducted workshops for patrons that include instruction in how to use Yahoo Groups? Broken out by total library budget.

	YES	NO
Less than $1,000,000	0.00%	100.00%
Between $1,000,000 - $5,000,000	2.70%	97.30%
Between $5,000,000 - $10,000,000	0.00%	100.00%
Over $10,000,000	0.00%	100.00%

Table 3.21:   Has the library ever conducted workshops for patrons that include instruction in how to use Flickr?

	YES	NO
Entire Sample	17.76%	82.24%

Table 3.22:   Has the library ever conducted workshops for patrons that include instruction in how to use Flickr? Broken out by type of library.

	YES	NO
Public Library	31.43%	68.57%
College/University Library	17.39%	82.61%
Law/Corporate Library	0.00%	100.00%
Government Agency/Department Library	0.00%	100.00%

Table 3.23:   Has the library ever conducted workshops for patrons that include instruction in how to use Flickr? Broken out by professional position at the library.

	YES	NO
Reference or Information Literacy	20.59%	79.41%
Research or Subject Specialist	15.38%	84.62%
Administration	18.18%	81.82%
Technical Services or Cataloging	14.29%	85.71%
Special Collections	0.00%	100.00%
Acquisitions or Collection Development	33.33%	66.67%

Table 3.24:   Has the library ever conducted workshops for patrons that include instruction in how to use Flickr? Broken out by total library budget

	YES	NO
Less than $1,000,000	7.89%	92.11%
Between $1,000,000 - $5,000,000	13.16%	86.84%
Between $5,000,000 - $10,000,000	25.00%	75.00%
Over $10,000,000	39.13%	60.87%

Table 3.25: Has the library ever conducted workshops for patrons that include instruction in how to use Tumblr?

	YES	NO
Entire Sample	0.00%	100.00%

Table 3.26: Has the library ever conducted workshops for patrons that include instruction in how to use LibraryThing?

	YES	NO
Entire Sample	5.61%	94.39%

Table 3.27: Has the library ever conducted workshops for patrons that include instruction in how to use LibraryThing? Broken out by type of library.

	YES	NO
Public Library	8.57%	91.43%
College/University Library	2.17%	97.83%
Law/Corporate Library	10.53%	89.47%
Government Agency/Department Library	0.00%	100.00%

Table 3.28: Has the library ever conducted workshops for patrons that include instruction in how to use LibraryThing? Broken out by professional position at the library.

	YES	NO
Reference or Information Literacy	5.88%	94.12%
Research or Subject Specialist	0.00%	100.00%
Administration	9.09%	90.91%
Technical Services or Cataloging	0.00%	100.00%
Special Collections	0.00%	100.00%
Acquisitions or Collection Development	0.00%	100.00%

Table 3.29:   Has the library ever conducted workshops for patrons that include instruction in how to use LibraryThing? Broken out by total library budget.

	YES	NO
Less than $1,000,000	2.63%	97.37%
Between $1,000,000 - $5,000,000	10.53%	89.47%
Between $5,000,000 - $10,000,000	0.00%	100.00%
Over $10,000,000	4.35%	95.65%

Table 3.30: Has the library ever conducted workshops for patrons that include instruction in how to use Yahoo Maps?

	YES	NO
Entire Sample	0.93%	99.07%

Table 3.31: Has the library ever conducted workshops for patrons that include instruction in how to use Yahoo Maps? Broken out by type of library.

	YES	NO
Public Library	2.86%	97.14%
College/University Library	0.00%	100.00%
Law/Corporate Library	0.00%	100.00%
Government Agency/Department Library	0.00%	100.00%

Table 3.32: Has the library ever conducted workshops for patrons that include instruction in how to use any Yahoo Maps? Broken out by professional position at the library.

	YES	NO
Reference or Information Literacy	0.00%	100.00%
Research or Subject Specialist	0.00%	100.00%
Administration	2.27%	97.73%
Technical Services or Cataloging	0.00%	100.00%
Special Collections	0.00%	100.00%
Acquisitions or Collection Development	0.00%	100.00%

Table 3.33: Has the library ever conducted workshops for patrons that include instruction in how to use Yahoo Maps? Broken out by total library budget.

	YES	NO
Less than $1,000,000	0.00%	100.00%
Between $1,000,000 - $5,000,000	0.00%	100.00%
Between $5,000,000 - $10,000,000	12.50%	87.50%
Over $10,000,000	0.00%	100.00%

Table 3.34: Has the library ever conducted workshops for patrons that include instruction in how to use the Bing search engine?

	YES	NO
Entire Sample	3.74%	96.26%

Table 3.35: Has the library ever conducted workshops for patrons that include instruction in how to use the Bing search engine? Broken out by type of library.

	YES	NO
Public Library	0.00%	100.00%
College/University Library	6.52%	93.48%
Law/Corporate Library	5.26%	94.74%
Government Agency/Department Library	0.00%	100.00%

Table 3.36: Has the library ever conducted workshops for patrons that include instruction in how to use the Bing search engine? Broken out by professional position at the library.

	YES	NO
Reference or Information Literacy	5.88%	94.12%
Research or Subject Specialist	0.00%	100.00%
Administration	2.27%	97.73%
Technical Services or Cataloging	0.00%	100.00%
Special Collections	20.00%	80.00%
Acquisitions or Collection Development	0.00%	100.00%

Table 3.37: Has the library ever conducted workshops for patrons that include instruction in how to use the Bing search engine? Broken out by total library budget.

	YES	NO
Less than $1,000,000	5.26%	94.74%
Between $1,000,000 - $5,000,000	5.26%	94.74%
Between $5,000,000 - $10,000,000	0.00%	100.00%
Over $10,000,000	0.00%	100.00%

Table 3.38: Has the library ever conducted workshops for patrons that include instruction in how to use the Google search engine?

	YES	NO
Entire Sample	43.93%	56.07%

Table 3.39: Has the library ever conducted workshops for patrons that include instruction in how to use The Google Search Engine? Broken out by type of library.

	YES	NO
Public Library	42.86%	57.14%
College/University Library	45.65%	54.35%
Law/Corporate Library	47.37%	52.63%
Government Agency/Department Library	28.57%	71.43%

Table 3.40: Has the library ever conducted workshops for patrons that include instruction in how to use the Google search engine? Broken out by professional position at the library.

	YES	NO
Reference or Information Literacy	50.00%	50.00%
Research or Subject Specialist	38.46%	61.54%
Administration	43.18%	56.82%
Technical Services or Cataloging	28.57%	71.43%
Special Collections	40.00%	60.00%
Acquisitions or Collection Development	66.67%	33.33%

Table 3.41: Has the library ever conducted workshops for patrons that include instruction in how to use the Google search engine? Broken out by total library budget.

	YES	NO
Less than $1,000,000	39.47%	60.53%
Between $1,000,000 - $5,000,000	47.37%	52.63%
Between $5,000,000 - $10,000,000	25.00%	75.00%
Over $10,000,000	52.17%	47.83%

Table 3.42: Has the library ever conducted workshops for patrons that include instruction in how to use YouTube?

	YES	NO
Entire Sample	10.28%	89.72%

Table 3.43: Has the library ever conducted workshops for patrons that include instruction in how to use YouTube? Broken out by type of library.

	YES	NO
Public Library	14.29%	85.71%
College/University Library	13.04%	86.96%
Law/Corporate Library	0.00%	100.00%
Government Agency/Department Library	0.00%	100.00%

Table 3.44: Has the library ever conducted workshops for patrons that include instruction in how to use YouTube? Broken out by professional position at the library.

	YES	NO
Reference or Information Literacy	14.71%	85.29%
Research or Subject Specialist	0.00%	100.00%
Administration	9.09%	90.91%
Technical Services or Cataloging	14.29%	85.71%
Special Collections	20.00%	80.00%
Acquisitions or Collection Development	0.00%	100.00%

Table 3.45: Has the library ever conducted workshops for patrons that include instruction in how to use YouTube? Broken out by total library budget.

	YES	NO
Less than $1,000,000	5.26%	94.74%
Between $1,000,000 - $5,000,000	13.16%	86.84%
Between $5,000,000 - $10,000,000	12.50%	87.50%
Over $10,000,000	13.04%	86.96%

Table 3.46:   Has the library ever conducted workshops for patrons that include instruction in how to use LinkedIn?

	YES	NO
Entire Sample	10.28%	89.72%

Table 3.47:   Has the library ever conducted workshops for patrons that include instruction in how to use LinkedIn? Broken out by type of library.

	YES	NO
Public Library	14.29%	85.71%
College/University Library	4.35%	95.65%
Law/Corporate Library	15.79%	84.21%
Government Agency/Department Library	14.29%	85.71%

Table 3.48:   Has the library ever conducted workshops for patrons that include instruction in how to use LinkedIn? Broken out by professional position at the library.

	YES	NO
Reference or Information Literacy	14.71%	85.29%
Research or Subject Specialist	7.69%	92.31%
Administration	9.09%	90.91%
Technical Services or Cataloging	14.29%	85.71%
Special Collections	0.00%	100.00%
Acquisitions or Collection Development	0.00%	100.00%

Table 3.49:   Has the library ever conducted workshops for patrons that include instruction in how to LinkedIn? Broken out by total library budget.

	YES	NO
Less than $1,000,000	7.89%	92.11%
Between $1,000,000 - $5,000,000	10.53%	89.47%
Between $5,000,000 - $10,000,000	0.00%	100.00%
Over $10,000,000	17.39%	82.61%

Table 3.50:   Has the library ever conducted workshops for patrons that include instruction in how to use Facebook?

	YES	NO
Entire Sample	29.91%	70.09%

Table 3.51:   Has the library ever conducted workshops for patrons that include instruction in how to use Facebook? Broken out by type of library.

	YES	NO
Public Library	60.00%	40.00%
College/University Library	17.39%	82.61%
Law/Corporate Library	10.53%	89.47%
Government Agency/Department Library	14.29%	85.71%

Table 3.52:   Has the library ever conducted workshops for patrons that include instruction in how to use Facebook? Broken out by professional position at the library.

	YES	NO
Reference or Information Literacy	38.24%	61.76%
Research or Subject Specialist	7.69%	92.31%
Administration	29.55%	70.45%
Technical Services or Cataloging	28.57%	71.43%
Special Collections	20.00%	80.00%
Acquisitions or Collection Development	66.67%	33.33%

Table 3.53:   Has the library ever conducted workshops for patrons that include instruction in how to use Facebook? Broken out by total library budget.

	YES	NO
Less than $1,000,000	13.16%	86.84%
Between $1,000,000 - $5,000,000	47.37%	52.63%
Between $5,000,000 - $10,000,000	25.00%	75.00%
Over $10,000,000	30.43%	69.57%

Table 3.54: Has the library ever conducted workshops for patrons that include instruction in how to use Blogger.com?

	YES	NO
Entire Sample	7.48%	92.52%

Table 3.55: Has the library ever conducted workshops for patrons that include instruction in how to use Blogger.com? Broken out by type of library.

	YES	NO
Public Library	8.57%	91.43%
College/University Library	6.52%	93.48%
Law/Corporate Library	5.26%	94.74%
Government Agency/Department Library	14.29%	85.71%

Table 3.56: Has the library ever conducted workshops for patrons that include instruction in how to use Blogger.com? Broken out by professional position at the library.

	YES	NO
Reference or Information Literacy	14.71%	85.29%
Research or Subject Specialist	7.69%	92.31%
Administration	4.55%	95.45%
Technical Services or Cataloging	0.00%	100.00%
Special Collections	0.00%	100.00%
Acquisitions or Collection Development	0.00%	100.00%

Table 3.57: Has the library ever conducted workshops for patrons that include instruction in how to use Blogger.com? Broken out by total library budget.

	YES	NO
Less than $1,000,000	5.26%	94.74%
Between $1,000,000 - $5,000,000	7.89%	92.11%
Between $5,000,000 - $10,000,000	12.50%	87.50%
Over $10,000,000	8.70%	91.30%

Table 3.58: Has the library ever conducted workshops for patrons that include instruction in how to use Twitter?

	YES	NO
Entire Sample	16.82%	83.18%

Table 3.59: Has the library ever conducted workshops for patrons that include instruction in how to use Twitter? Broken out by type of library.

	YES	NO
Public Library	31.43%	68.57%
College/University Library	8.70%	91.30%
Law/Corporate Library	5.26%	94.74%
Government Agency/Department Library	28.57%	71.43%

Table 3.60: Has the library ever conducted workshops for patrons that include instruction in how to use Twitter? Broken out by professional position at the library.

	YES	NO
Reference or Information Literacy	23.53%	76.47%
Research or Subject Specialist	15.38%	84.62%
Administration	15.91%	84.09%
Technical Services or Cataloging	0.00%	100.00%
Special Collections	0.00%	100.00%
Acquisitions or Collection Development	33.33%	66.67%

Table 3.61: Has the library ever conducted workshops for patrons that include instruction in how to use Twitter? Broken out by total library budget.

	YES	NO
Less than $1,000,000	7.89%	92.11%
Between $1,000,000 - $5,000,000	21.05%	78.95%
Between $5,000,000 - $10,000,000	12.50%	87.50%
Over $10,000,000	26.09%	73.91%

Table 3.62: Has the library ever conducted workshops for patrons that include instruction in how to use Wordpress.com?

	YES	NO
Entire Sample	8.41%	91.59%

Table 3.63: Has the library ever conducted workshops for patrons that include instruction in how to use Wordpress.com? Broken out by type of library.

	YES	NO
Public Library	2.86%	97.14%
College/University Library	15.22%	84.78%
Law/Corporate Library	5.26%	94.74%
Government Agency/Department Library	0.00%	100.00%

Table 3.64: Has the library ever conducted workshops for patrons that include instruction in how to use Wordpress.com? Broken out by professional position at the library.

	YES	NO
Reference or Information Literacy	14.71%	85.29%
Research or Subject Specialist	0.00%	100.00%
Administration	4.55%	95.45%
Technical Services or Cataloging	0.00%	100.00%
Special Collections	20.00%	80.00%
Acquisitions or Collection Development	33.33%	66.67%

Table 3.65: Has the library ever conducted workshops for patrons that include instruction in how to use Wordpress.com? Broken out by total library budget.

	YES	NO
Less than $1,000,000	7.89%	92.11%
Between $1,000,000 - $5,000,000	10.53%	89.47%
Between $5,000,000 - $10,000,000	0.00%	100.00%
Over $10,000,000	8.70%	91.30%

4. Usefulness of Various Internet Sites

Table 4.1: Rate the usefulness of Google Books in your professional library work.

	HIGHLY USEFUL	USEFUL	OCCASIONALLY USEFUL	NOT VERY USEFUL	DO NOT USE/DON'T KNOW
Entire Sample	16.19%	21.90%	35.24%	12.38%	14.29%

Table 4.2: Rate the usefulness of Google Books in your professional library work. Broken out by type of library.

	HIGHLY USEFUL	USEFUL	OCCASIONALLY USEFUL	NOT VERY USEFUL	DO NOT USE/DON'T KNOW
Public Library	8.82%	11.76%	35.29%	23.53%	20.59%
College/University Library	22.22%	35.56%	31.11%	2.22%	8.89%
Law/Corporate Library	10.53%	15.79%	47.37%	15.79%	10.53%
Government Agency/Department Library	28.57%	0.00%	28.57%	14.29%	28.57%

Table 4.3: Rate the usefulness of Google Books in your professional library work. Broken out by professional position at the library.

	HIGHLY USEFUL	USEFUL	OCCASIONALLY USEFUL	NOT VERY USEFUL	DO NOT USE/DON'T KNOW
Reference or Information Literacy	24.24%	24.24%	27.27%	12.12%	12.12%
Research or Subject Specialist	38.46%	7.69%	38.46%	7.69%	7.69%
Administration	0.00%	20.93%	44.19%	16.28%	18.60%
Technical Services or Cataloging	14.29%	28.57%	28.57%	0.00%	28.57%
Special Collections	20.00%	60.00%	20.00%	0.00%	0.00%
Acquisitions or Collection Development	66.67%	0.00%	0.00%	33.33%	0.00%

Table 4.4: Rate the usefulness of Google Books in your professional library work. Broken out by total library budget.

	HIGHLY USEFUL	USEFUL	OCCASIONALLY USEFUL	NOT VERY USEFUL	DO NOT USE/DON'T KNOW
Less than $1,000,000	13.16%	21.05%	31.58%	18.42%	15.79%
Between $1,000,000 - $5,000,000	16.22%	10.81%	45.95%	10.81%	16.22%
Between $5,000,000 - $10,000,000	25.00%	25.00%	25.00%	0.00%	25.00%
Over $10,000,000	18.18%	40.91%	27.27%	9.09%	4.55%

Table 4.5: Rate the usefulness of Google Maps in your professional library work.

	HIGHLY USEFUL	USEFUL	OCCASIONALLY USEFUL	NOT VERY USEFUL	DO NOT USE/DON'T KNOW
Entire Sample	21.15%	31.73%	29.81%	11.54%	5.77%

Table 4.6: Rate the usefulness of Google Maps in your professional library work. Broken out by type of library.

	HIGHLY USEFUL	USEFUL	OCCASIONALLY USEFUL	NOT VERY USEFUL	DO NOT USE/DON'T KNOW
Public Library	32.35%	35.29%	23.53%	0.00%	8.82%
College/University Library	15.91%	34.09%	34.09%	13.64%	2.27%
Law/Corporate Library	10.53%	15.79%	42.11%	21.05%	10.53%
Government Agency/Department Library	28.57%	42.86%	0.00%	28.57%	0.00%

Table 4.7: Rate the usefulness of Google Maps in your professional library work. Broken out by professional position at the library.

	HIGHLY USEFUL	USEFUL	OCCASIONALLY USEFUL	NOT VERY USEFUL	DO NOT USE/DON'T KNOW
Reference or Information Literacy	18.18%	33.33%	30.30%	12.12%	6.06%
Research or Subject Specialist	15.38%	30.77%	7.69%	46.15%	0.00%
Administration	23.26%	25.58%	41.86%	2.33%	6.98%
Technical Services or Cataloging	28.57%	42.86%	0.00%	14.29%	14.29%
Special Collections	50.00%	50.00%	0.00%	0.00%	0.00%
Acquisitions or Collection Development	0.00%	66.67%	33.33%	0.00%	0.00%

Table 4.8:   Rate the usefulness of Google Maps in your professional library work. Broken out by total library budget.

	HIGHLY USEFUL	USEFUL	OCCASIONALLY USEFUL	NOT VERY USEFUL	DO NOT USE/DON'T KNOW
Less than $1,000,000	21.62%	27.03%	35.14%	8.11%	8.11%
Between $1,000,000 - $5,000,000	18.92%	32.43%	35.14%	10.81%	2.70%
Between $5,000,000 - $10,000,000	0.00%	25.00%	37.50%	25.00%	12.50%
Over $10,000,000	31.82%	40.91%	9.09%	13.64%	4.55%

Table 4.9: Rate the usefulness of Google RealTime in your professional library work.

	HIGHLY USEFUL	USEFUL	OCCASIONALLY USEFUL	NOT VERY USEFUL	DO NOT USE/DON'T KNOW
Entire Sample	2.91%	1.94%	5.83%	12.62%	76.70%

Table 4.10: Rate the usefulness of Google RealTime in your professional library work. Broken out by type of library.

	HIGHLY USEFUL	USEFUL	OCCASIONALLY USEFUL	NOT VERY USEFUL	DO NOT USE/DON'T KNOW
Public Library	2.94%	0.00%	5.88%	14.71%	76.47%
College/University Library	2.33%	2.33%	6.98%	6.98%	81.40%
Law/Corporate Library	5.26%	5.26%	0.00%	26.32%	63.16%
Government Agency/Department Library	0.00%	0.00%	14.29%	0.00%	85.71%

Table 4.11: Rate the usefulness of Google RealTime in your professional library work. Broken out by professional position at the library.

	HIGHLY USEFUL	USEFUL	OCCASIONALLY USEFUL	NOT VERY USEFUL	DO NOT USE/DON'T KNOW
Reference or Information Literacy	6.06%	3.03%	3.03%	9.09%	78.79%
Research or Subject Specialist	7.69%	0.00%	15.38%	7.69%	69.23%
Administration	0.00%	2.33%	6.98%	18.60%	72.09%
Technical Services or Cataloging	0.00%	0.00%	0.00%	0.00%	100.00%
Special Collections	0.00%	0.00%	0.00%	0.00%	100.00%
Acquisitions or Collection Development	0.00%	0.00%	0.00%	33.33%	66.67%

Table 4.12: Rate the usefulness of Google RealTime in your professional library work. Broken out by total library budget.

	HIGHLY USEFUL	USEFUL	OCCASIONALLY USEFUL	NOT VERY USEFUL	DO NOT USE/DON'T KNOW
Less than $1,000,000	2.70%	0.00%	5.41%	13.51%	78.38%
Between $1,000,000 - $5,000,000	2.78%	0.00%	8.33%	16.67%	72.22%
Between $5,000,000 - $10,000,000	0.00%	12.50%	0.00%	12.50%	75.00%
Over $10,000,000	4.55%	4.55%	4.55%	4.55%	81.82%

Table 4.13: Rate the usefulness of Google Translate in your professional library work.

	HIGHLY USEFUL	USEFUL	OCCASIONALLY USEFUL	NOT VERY USEFUL	DO NOT USE/DON'T KNOW
Entire Sample	8.74%	16.50%	38.83%	13.59%	22.33%

Table 4.14: Rate the usefulness of Google Translate in your professional library work. Broken out by type of library.

	HIGHLY USEFUL	USEFUL	OCCASIONALLY USEFUL	NOT VERY USEFUL	DO NOT USE/DON'T KNOW
Public Library	2.94%	20.59%	32.35%	11.76%	32.35%
College/University Library	9.30%	11.63%	39.53%	18.60%	20.93%
Law/Corporate Library	10.53%	21.05%	42.11%	10.53%	15.79%
Government Agency/Department Library	28.57%	14.29%	57.14%	0.00%	0.00%

Table 4.15: Rate the usefulness of Google Translate in your professional library work. Broken out by professional position at the library.

	HIGHLY USEFUL	USEFUL	OCCASIONALLY USEFUL	NOT VERY USEFUL	DO NOT USE/DON'T KNOW
Reference or Information Literacy	9.38%	15.63%	37.50%	12.50%	25.00%
Research or Subject Specialist	23.08%	7.69%	46.15%	15.38%	7.69%
Administration	2.33%	23.26%	37.21%	16.28%	20.93%
Technical Services or Cataloging	0.00%	14.29%	28.57%	14.29%	42.86%
Special Collections	25.00%	0.00%	25.00%	0.00%	50.00%
Acquisitions or Collection Development	33.33%	0.00%	66.67%	0.00%	0.00%

Table 4.16: Rate the usefulness of Google Translate in your professional library work. Broken out by total library budget.

	HIGHLY USEFUL	USEFUL	OCCASIONALLY USEFUL	NOT VERY USEFUL	DO NOT USE/DON'T KNOW
Less than $1,000,000	8.33%	13.89%	44.44%	13.89%	19.44%
Between $1,000,000 - $5,000,000	5.41%	18.92%	35.14%	10.81%	29.73%
Between $5,000,000 - $10,000,000	0.00%	25.00%	12.50%	25.00%	37.50%
Over $10,000,000	18.18%	13.64%	45.45%	13.64%	9.09%

Table 4.17:   Rate the usefulness of Google Scholar in your professional library work.

	HIGHLY USEFUL	USEFUL	OCCASIONALLY USEFUL	NOT VERY USEFUL	DO NOT USE/DON'T KNOW
Entire Sample	29.25%	23.58%	24.53%	7.55%	15.09%

Table 4.18:   Rate the usefulness of Google Scholar in your professional library work. Broken out by type of library.

	HIGHLY USEFUL	USEFUL	OCCASIONALLY USEFUL	NOT VERY USEFUL	DO NOT USE/DON'T KNOW
Public Library	5.88%	8.82%	44.12%	11.76%	29.41%
College/University Library	41.30%	39.13%	10.87%	2.17%	6.52%
Law/Corporate Library	42.11%	15.79%	26.32%	5.26%	10.53%
Government Agency/Department Library	28.57%	14.29%	14.29%	28.57%	14.29%

Table 4.19:   Rate the usefulness of Google Scholar in your professional library work. Broken out by professional position at the library.

	HIGHLY USEFUL	USEFUL	OCCASIONALLY USEFUL	NOT VERY USEFUL	DO NOT USE/DON'T KNOW
Reference or Information Literacy	38.24%	23.53%	20.59%	8.82%	8.82%
Research or Subject Specialist	38.46%	38.46%	15.38%	7.69%	0.00%
Administration	20.93%	20.93%	32.56%	6.98%	18.60%
Technical Services or Cataloging	28.57%	14.29%	14.29%	0.00%	42.86%
Special Collections	20.00%	20.00%	20.00%	0.00%	40.00%
Acquisitions or Collection Development	33.33%	0.00%	33.33%	33.33%	0.00%

Table 4.20: Rate the usefulness of Google Scholar in your professional library work. Broken out by total library budget.

	HIGHLY USEFUL	USEFUL	OCCASIONALLY USEFUL	NOT VERY USEFUL	DO NOT USE/DON'T KNOW
Less than $1,000,000	23.68%	23.68%	23.68%	10.53%	18.42%
Between $1,000,000 - $5,000,000	29.73%	16.22%	32.43%	5.41%	16.22%
Between $5,000,000 - $10,000,000	37.50%	12.50%	25.00%	12.50%	12.50%
Over $10,000,000	34.78%	39.13%	13.04%	4.35%	8.70%

Table 4.21:   Rate the usefulness of Google Buzz in your professional library work.

	HIGHLY USEFUL	USEFUL	OCCASIONALLY USEFUL	NOT VERY USEFUL	DO NOT USE/DON'T KNOW
Entire Sample	2.97%	0.99%	3.96%	20.79%	71.29%

Table 4.22:   Rate the usefulness of Google Buzz in your professional library work. Broken out by type of library.

	HIGHLY USEFUL	USEFUL	OCCASIONALLY USEFUL	NOT VERY USEFUL	DO NOT USE/DON'T KNOW
Public Library	2.94%	2.94%	8.82%	14.71%	70.59%
College/University Library	4.76%	0.00%	2.38%	19.05%	73.81%
Law/Corporate Library	0.00%	0.00%	0.00%	27.78%	72.22%
Government Agency/Department Library	0.00%	0.00%	0.00%	42.86%	57.14%

Table 4.23:   Rate the usefulness of Google Buzz in your professional library work. Broken out by professional position at the library.

	HIGHLY USEFUL	USEFUL	OCCASIONALLY USEFUL	NOT VERY USEFUL	DO NOT USE/DON'T KNOW
Reference or Information Literacy	9.09%	0.00%	0.00%	18.18%	72.73%
Research or Subject Specialist	0.00%	0.00%	8.33%	50.00%	41.67%
Administration	0.00%	2.38%	7.14%	11.90%	78.57%
Technical Services or Cataloging	0.00%	0.00%	0.00%	28.57%	71.43%
Special Collections	0.00%	0.00%	0.00%	33.33%	66.67%
Acquisitions or Collection Development	0.00%	0.00%	0.00%	33.33%	66.67%

Table 4.24:   Rate the usefulness of Google Buzz in your professional library work. Broken out by total library budget.

	HIGHLY USEFUL	USEFUL	OCCASIONALLY USEFUL	NOT VERY USEFUL	DO NOT USE/DON'T KNOW
Less than $1,000,000	2.70%	0.00%	0.00%	18.92%	78.38%
Between $1,000,000 - $5,000,000	2.86%	0.00%	8.57%	14.29%	74.29%
Between $5,000,000 - $10,000,000	0.00%	0.00%	0.00%	12.50%	87.50%
Over $10,000,000	4.76%	4.76%	4.76%	38.10%	47.62%

Table 4.25: Rate the usefulness of Yahoo Groups in your professional
library work.

	HIGHLY USEFUL	USEFUL	OCCASIONALLY USEFUL	NOT VERY USEFUL	DO NOT USE/DON'T KNOW
Entire Sample	0.00%	9.80%	16.67%	28.43%	45.10%

Table 4.26: Rate the usefulness of Yahoo Groups in your professional
library work. Broken out by type of library.

	HIGHLY USEFUL	USEFUL	OCCASIONALLY USEFUL	NOT VERY USEFUL	DO NOT USE/DON'T KNOW
Public Library	0.00%	11.76%	26.47%	17.65%	44.12%
College/University Library	0.00%	7.14%	9.52%	38.10%	45.24%
Law/Corporate Library	0.00%	5.26%	5.26%	26.32%	63.16%
Government Agency/Department Library	0.00%	28.57%	42.86%	28.57%	0.00%

Table 4.27: Rate the usefulness of Yahoo Groups in your professional
library work. Broken out by professional position at the library.

	HIGHLY USEFUL	USEFUL	OCCASIONALLY USEFUL	NOT VERY USEFUL	DO NOT USE/DON'T KNOW
Reference or Information Literacy	0.00%	9.38%	12.50%	34.38%	43.75%
Research or Subject Specialist	0.00%	23.08%	15.38%	38.46%	23.08%
Administration	0.00%	9.30%	23.26%	18.60%	48.84%
Technical Services or Cataloging	0.00%	0.00%	14.29%	28.57%	57.14%
Special Collections	0.00%	0.00%	0.00%	33.33%	66.67%
Acquisitions or Collection Development	0.00%	0.00%	0.00%	66.67%	33.33%

Table 4.28: Rate the usefulness of Yahoo Groups in your professional library work. Broken out by total library budget.

	HIGHLY USEFUL	USEFUL	OCCASIONALLY USEFUL	NOT VERY USEFUL	DO NOT USE/DON'T KNOW
Less than $1,000,000	0.00%	13.89%	13.89%	27.78%	44.44%
Between $1,000,000 - $5,000,000	0.00%	5.56%	22.22%	25.00%	47.22%
Between $5,000,000 - $10,000,000	0.00%	12.50%	12.50%	12.50%	62.50%
Over $10,000,000	0.00%	9.09%	13.64%	40.91%	36.36%

Table 4.29: Rate the usefulness of Flickr in your professional library work.

	HIGHLY USEFUL	USEFUL	OCCASIONALLY USEFUL	NOT VERY USEFUL	DO NOT USE/DON'T KNOW
Entire Sample	5.66%	16.04%	26.42%	25.47%	26.42%

Table 4.30: Rate the usefulness of Flickr in your professional library work. Broken out by type of library.

	HIGHLY USEFUL	USEFUL	OCCASIONALLY USEFUL	NOT VERY USEFUL	DO NOT USE/DON'T KNOW
Public Library	8.57%	28.57%	22.86%	11.43%	28.57%
College/University Library	6.67%	11.11%	33.33%	33.33%	15.56%
Law/Corporate Library	0.00%	5.26%	5.26%	31.58%	57.89%
Government Agency/Department Library	0.00%	14.29%	57.14%	28.57%	0.00%

Table 4.31: Rate the usefulness of Flickr in your professional library work. Broken out by professional position at the library.

	HIGHLY USEFUL	USEFUL	OCCASIONALLY USEFUL	NOT VERY USEFUL	DO NOT USE/DON'T KNOW
Reference or Information Literacy	8.82%	14.71%	23.53%	23.53%	29.41%
Research or Subject Specialist	0.00%	15.38%	38.46%	46.15%	0.00%
Administration	6.82%	20.45%	25.00%	15.91%	31.82%
Technical Services or Cataloging	0.00%	14.29%	42.86%	0.00%	42.86%
Special Collections	0.00%	0.00%	0.00%	75.00%	25.00%
Acquisitions or Collection Development	0.00%	0.00%	33.33%	66.67%	0.00%

Table 4.32:   Rate the usefulness of Flickr in your professional library work. Broken out by total library budget.

	HIGHLY USEFUL	USEFUL	OCCASIONALLY USEFUL	NOT VERY USEFUL	DO NOT USE/DON'T KNOW
Less than $1,000,000	5.41%	13.51%	32.43%	16.22%	32.43%
Between $1,000,000 - $5,000,000	7.89%	10.53%	13.16%	34.21%	34.21%
Between $5,000,000 - $10,000,000	0.00%	12.50%	37.50%	25.00%	25.00%
Over $10,000,000	4.35%	30.43%	34.78%	26.09%	4.35%

Table 4.33: Rate the usefulness of Tumblr in your professional library work.

	HIGHLY USEFUL	USEFUL	OCCASIONALLY USEFUL	NOT VERY USEFUL	DO NOT USE/DON'T KNOW
Entire Sample	0.00%	4.85%	6.80%	23.30%	65.05%

Table 4.34: Rate the usefulness of Tumblr in your professional library work. Broken out by type of library.

	HIGHLY USEFUL	USEFUL	OCCASIONALLY USEFUL	NOT VERY USEFUL	DO NOT USE/DON'T KNOW
Public Library	0.00%	5.88%	8.82%	17.65%	67.65%
College/University Library	0.00%	6.98%	4.65%	20.93%	67.44%
Law/Corporate Library	0.00%	0.00%	0.00%	31.58%	68.42%
Government Agency/Department Library	0.00%	0.00%	28.57%	42.86%	28.57%

Table 4.35: Rate the usefulness of Tumblr in your professional library work. Broken out by professional position at the library.

	HIGHLY USEFUL	USEFUL	OCCASIONALLY USEFUL	NOT VERY USEFUL	DO NOT USE/DON'T KNOW
Reference or Information Literacy	0.00%	9.09%	9.09%	21.21%	60.61%
Research or Subject Specialist	0.00%	0.00%	7.69%	53.85%	38.46%
Administration	0.00%	4.65%	4.65%	16.28%	74.42%
Technical Services or Cataloging	0.00%	0.00%	14.29%	14.29%	71.43%
Special Collections	0.00%	0.00%	0.00%	0.00%	100.00%
Acquisitions or Collection Development	0.00%	0.00%	0.00%	33.33%	66.67%

Table 4.36: Rate the usefulness of Tumblr in your professional library work. Broken out by total library budget.

	HIGHLY USEFUL	USEFUL	OCCASIONALLY USEFUL	NOT VERY USEFUL	DO NOT USE/DON'T KNOW
Less than $1,000,000	0.00%	0.00%	5.56%	16.67%	77.78%
Between $1,000,000 - $5,000,000	0.00%	2.78%	8.33%	30.56%	58.33%
Between $5,000,000 - $10,000,000	0.00%	0.00%	0.00%	12.50%	87.50%
Over $10,000,000	0.00%	17.39%	8.70%	26.09%	47.83%

Table 4.37:   Rate the usefulness of LibraryThing in your professional library work.

	HIGHLY USEFUL	USEFUL	OCCASIONALLY USEFUL	NOT VERY USEFUL	DO NOT USE/DON'T KNOW
Entire Sample	4.04%	10.10%	20.20%	26.26%	39.39%

Table 4.38:   Rate the usefulness of LibraryThing in your professional library work. Broken out by type of library.

	HIGHLY USEFUL	USEFUL	OCCASIONALLY USEFUL	NOT VERY USEFUL	DO NOT USE/DON'T KNOW
Public Library	9.38%	18.75%	18.75%	18.75%	34.38%
College/University Library	0.00%	4.88%	26.83%	34.15%	34.15%
Law/Corporate Library	5.26%	5.26%	5.26%	21.05%	63.16%
Government Agency/Department Library	0.00%	14.29%	28.57%	28.57%	28.57%

Table 4.39:   Rate the usefulness of LibraryThing in your professional library work. Broken out by professional position at the library.

	HIGHLY USEFUL	USEFUL	OCCASIONALLY USEFUL	NOT VERY USEFUL	DO NOT USE/DON'T KNOW
Reference or Information Literacy	0.00%	6.45%	19.35%	22.58%	51.61%
Research or Subject Specialist	0.00%	7.69%	7.69%	53.85%	30.77%
Administration	9.52%	11.90%	19.05%	21.43%	38.10%
Technical Services or Cataloging	0.00%	0.00%	42.86%	14.29%	42.86%
Special Collections	0.00%	50.00%	50.00%	0.00%	0.00%
Acquisitions or Collection Development	0.00%	33.33%	33.33%	33.33%	0.00%

Table 4.40: Rate the usefulness of LibraryThing in your professional library work. Broken out by total library budget.

	HIGHLY USEFUL	USEFUL	OCCASIONALLY USEFUL	NOT VERY USEFUL	DO NOT USE/DON'T KNOW
Less than $1,000,000	5.56%	8.33%	19.44%	22.22%	44.44%
Between $1,000,000 - $5,000,000	5.71%	8.57%	22.86%	17.14%	45.71%
Between $5,000,000 - $10,000,000	0.00%	12.50%	0.00%	37.50%	50.00%
Over $10,000,000	0.00%	15.00%	25.00%	45.00%	15.00%

Table 4.41: Rate the usefulness of Yahoo Maps in your professional library work.

	HIGHLY USEFUL	USEFUL	OCCASIONALLY USEFUL	NOT VERY USEFUL	DO NOT USE/DON'T KNOW
Entire Sample	2.91%	17.48%	24.27%	21.36%	33.98%

Table 4.42: Rate the usefulness of Yahoo Maps in your professional library work. Broken out by type of library.

	HIGHLY USEFUL	USEFUL	OCCASIONALLY USEFUL	NOT VERY USEFUL	DO NOT USE/DON'T KNOW
Public Library	5.88%	20.59%	23.53%	20.59%	29.41%
College/University Library	2.33%	13.95%	27.91%	20.93%	34.88%
Law/Corporate Library	0.00%	5.26%	26.32%	26.32%	42.11%
Government Agency/Department Library	0.00%	57.14%	0.00%	14.29%	28.57%

Table 4.43: Rate the usefulness of Yahoo Maps in your professional library work. Broken out by professional position at the library.

	HIGHLY USEFUL	USEFUL	OCCASIONALLY USEFUL	NOT VERY USEFUL	DO NOT USE/DON'T KNOW
Reference or Information Literacy	0.00%	18.75%	25.00%	18.75%	37.50%
Research or Subject Specialist	7.69%	15.38%	0.00%	46.15%	30.77%
Administration	4.55%	13.64%	34.09%	15.91%	31.82%
Technical Services or Cataloging	0.00%	28.57%	14.29%	14.29%	42.86%
Special Collections	0.00%	50.00%	0.00%	25.00%	25.00%
Acquisitions or Collection Development	0.00%	0.00%	0.00%	50.00%	50.00%

Table 4.44: Rate the usefulness of Yahoo Maps in your professional library work. Broken out by total library budget.

	HIGHLY USEFUL	USEFUL	OCCASIONALLY USEFUL	NOT VERY USEFUL	DO NOT USE/DON'T KNOW
Less than $1,000,000	0.00%	19.44%	22.22%	13.89%	44.44%
Between $1,000,000 - $5,000,000	2.70%	24.32%	32.43%	13.51%	27.03%
Between $5,000,000 - $10,000,000	0.00%	0.00%	12.50%	37.50%	50.00%
Over $10,000,000	9.09%	9.09%	18.18%	40.91%	22.73%

Table 4.45: Rate the usefulness of the Bing search engine in your professional library work.

	HIGHLY USEFUL	USEFUL	OCCASIONALLY USEFUL	NOT VERY USEFUL	DO NOT USE/DON'T KNOW
Entire Sample	5.77%	14.42%	27.88%	20.19%	31.73%

Table 4.46: Rate the usefulness of the Bing search engine in your professional library work. Broken out by type of library.

	HIGHLY USEFUL	USEFUL	OCCASIONALLY USEFUL	NOT VERY USEFUL	DO NOT USE/DON'T KNOW
Public Library	5.88%	11.76%	17.65%	26.47%	38.24%
College/University Library	4.55%	13.64%	34.09%	20.45%	27.27%
Law/Corporate Library	5.26%	21.05%	31.58%	10.53%	31.58%
Government Agency/Department Library	14.29%	14.29%	28.57%	14.29%	28.57%

Table 4.47: Rate the usefulness of the Bing search engine in your professional library work. Broken out by professional position at the library.

	HIGHLY USEFUL	USEFUL	OCCASIONALLY USEFUL	NOT VERY USEFUL	DO NOT USE/DON'T KNOW
Reference or Information Literacy	6.06%	9.09%	27.27%	21.21%	36.36%
Research or Subject Specialist	7.69%	15.38%	23.08%	23.08%	30.77%
Administration	6.98%	18.60%	27.91%	18.60%	27.91%
Technical Services or Cataloging	0.00%	0.00%	42.86%	0.00%	57.14%
Special Collections	0.00%	50.00%	25.00%	0.00%	25.00%
Acquisitions or Collection Development	0.00%	0.00%	0.00%	100.00%	0.00%

Table 4.48: Rate the usefulness of the Bing search engine in your professional library work. Broken out by total library budget.

	HIGHLY USEFUL	USEFUL	OCCASIONALLY USEFUL	NOT VERY USEFUL	DO NOT USE/DON'T KNOW
Less than $1,000,000	13.51%	13.51%	24.32%	10.81%	37.84%
Between $1,000,000 - $5,000,000	0.00%	16.22%	37.84%	16.22%	29.73%
Between $5,000,000 - $10,000,000	0.00%	12.50%	12.50%	37.50%	37.50%
Over $10,000,000	4.55%	13.64%	22.73%	36.36%	22.73%

Table 4.49:   Rate the usefulness of the Google search engine in your professional library work.

	HIGHLY USEFUL	USEFUL	OCCASIONALLY USEFUL	NOT VERY USEFUL	DO NOT USE/DON'T KNOW
Entire Sample	71.70%	20.75%	4.72%	0.00%	2.83%

Table 4.50:   Rate the usefulness of the Google search engine in your professional library work. Broken out by type of library.

	HIGHLY USEFUL	USEFUL	OCCASIONALLY USEFUL	NOT VERY USEFUL	DO NOT USE/DON'T KNOW
Public Library	68.57%	22.86%	2.86%	0.00%	5.71%
College/University Library	71.11%	24.44%	4.44%	0.00%	0.00%
Law/Corporate Library	78.95%	10.53%	5.26%	0.00%	5.26%
Government Agency/Department Library	71.43%	14.29%	14.29%	0.00%	0.00%

Table 4.51:   Rate the usefulness of the Google search engine in your professional library work. Broken out by professional position at the library.

	HIGHLY USEFUL	USEFUL	OCCASIONALLY USEFUL	NOT VERY USEFUL	DO NOT USE/DON'T KNOW
Reference or Information Literacy	72.73%	24.24%	0.00%	0.00%	3.03%
Research or Subject Specialist	61.54%	23.08%	15.38%	0.00%	0.00%
Administration	70.45%	18.18%	6.82%	0.00%	4.55%
Technical Services or Cataloging	71.43%	28.57%	0.00%	0.00%	0.00%
Special Collections	100.00%	0.00%	0.00%	0.00%	0.00%
Acquisitions or Collection Development	100.00%	0.00%	0.00%	0.00%	0.00%

Table 4.52:   Rate the usefulness of the Google search engine in your professional library work. Broken out by total library budget.

	HIGHLY USEFUL	USEFUL	OCCASIONALLY USEFUL	NOT VERY USEFUL	DO NOT USE/DON'T KNOW
Less than $1,000,000	68.42%	15.79%	7.89%	0.00%	7.89%
Between $1,000,000 - $5,000,000	71.05%	28.95%	0.00%	0.00%	0.00%
Between $5,000,000 - $10,000,000	75.00%	25.00%	0.00%	0.00%	0.00%
Over $10,000,000	77.27%	13.64%	9.09%	0.00%	0.00%

Table 4.53: Rate the usefulness of LinkedIn in your professional library work.

	HIGHLY USEFUL	USEFUL	OCCASIONALLY USEFUL	NOT VERY USEFUL	DO NOT USE/DON'T KNOW
Entire Sample	9.43%	16.04%	23.58%	29.25%	21.70%

Table 4.54: Rate the usefulness of LinkedIn in your professional library work. Broken out by type of library.

	HIGHLY USEFUL	USEFUL	OCCASIONALLY USEFUL	NOT VERY USEFUL	DO NOT USE/DON'T KNOW
Public Library	2.86%	17.14%	37.14%	22.86%	20.00%
College/University Library	4.44%	8.89%	17.78%	42.22%	26.67%
Law/Corporate Library	26.32%	31.58%	15.79%	15.79%	10.53%
Government Agency/Department Library	28.57%	14.29%	14.29%	14.29%	28.57%

Table 4.55: Rate the usefulness of LinkedIn in your professional library work. Broken out by professional position at the library.

	HIGHLY USEFUL	USEFUL	OCCASIONALLY USEFUL	NOT VERY USEFUL	DO NOT USE/DON'T KNOW
Reference or Information Literacy	5.88%	17.65%	8.82%	35.29%	32.35%
Research or Subject Specialist	15.38%	7.69%	15.38%	30.77%	30.77%
Administration	13.64%	18.18%	34.09%	22.73%	11.36%
Technical Services or Cataloging	0.00%	0.00%	42.86%	42.86%	14.29%
Special Collections	0.00%	0.00%	50.00%	0.00%	50.00%
Acquisitions or Collection Development	0.00%	66.67%	0.00%	33.33%	0.00%

Table 4.56: Rate the usefulness of LinkedIn in your professional library work. Broken out by total library budget.

	HIGHLY USEFUL	USEFUL	OCCASIONALLY USEFUL	NOT VERY USEFUL	DO NOT USE/DON'T KNOW
Less than $1,000,000	16.22%	8.11%	24.32%	32.43%	18.92%
Between $1,000,000 - $5,000,000	5.26%	21.05%	28.95%	21.05%	23.68%
Between $5,000,000 - $10,000,000	25.00%	0.00%	12.50%	25.00%	37.50%
Over $10,000,000	0.00%	26.09%	17.39%	39.13%	17.39%

Table 4.57:   Rate the usefulness of YouTube in your professional library work.

	HIGHLY USEFUL	USEFUL	OCCASIONALLY USEFUL	NOT VERY USEFUL	DO NOT USE/DON'T KNOW
Entire Sample	16.04%	26.42%	36.79%	11.32%	9.43%

Table 4.58:   Rate the usefulness of YouTube in your professional library work. Broken out by type of library.

	HIGHLY USEFUL	USEFUL	OCCASIONALLY USEFUL	NOT VERY USEFUL	DO NOT USE/DON'T KNOW
Public Library	8.57%	34.29%	42.86%	8.57%	5.71%
College/University Library	20.00%	28.89%	35.56%	6.67%	8.89%
Law/Corporate Library	15.79%	10.53%	26.32%	26.32%	21.05%
Government Agency/Department Library	28.57%	14.29%	42.86%	14.29%	0.00%

Table 4.59:   Rate the usefulness of YouTube in your professional library work. Broken out by professional position at the library.

	HIGHLY USEFUL	USEFUL	OCCASIONALLY USEFUL	NOT VERY USEFUL	DO NOT USE/DON'T KNOW
Reference or Information Literacy	17.65%	35.29%	35.29%	5.88%	5.88%
Research or Subject Specialist	23.08%	0.00%	38.46%	23.08%	15.38%
Administration	13.64%	25.00%	36.36%	15.91%	9.09%
Technical Services or Cataloging	0.00%	28.57%	42.86%	0.00%	28.57%
Special Collections	0.00%	50.00%	50.00%	0.00%	0.00%
Acquisitions or Collection Development	66.67%	33.33%	0.00%	0.00%	0.00%

Table 4.60: Rate the usefulness of YouTube in your professional library work. Broken out by total library budget.

	HIGHLY USEFUL	USEFUL	OCCASIONALLY USEFUL	NOT VERY USEFUL	DO NOT USE/DON'T KNOW
Less than $1,000,000	21.62%	16.22%	35.14%	13.51%	13.51%
Between $1,000,000 - $5,000,000	10.53%	31.58%	36.84%	13.16%	7.89%
Between $5,000,000 - $10,000,000	0.00%	25.00%	62.50%	12.50%	0.00%
Over $10,000,000	21.74%	34.78%	30.43%	4.35%	8.70%

Table 4.61: Rate the usefulness of Wikipedia in your professional library work.

	HIGHLY USEFUL	USEFUL	OCCASIONALLY USEFUL	NOT VERY USEFUL	DO NOT USE/DON'T KNOW
Entire Sample	25.71%	40.95%	20.95%	5.71%	6.67%

Table 4.62: Rate the usefulness of Wikipedia in your professional library work. Broken out by type of library.

	HIGHLY USEFUL	USEFUL	OCCASIONALLY USEFUL	NOT VERY USEFUL	DO NOT USE/DON'T KNOW
Public Library	20.59%	44.12%	26.47%	0.00%	8.82%
College/University Library	26.67%	42.22%	20.00%	6.67%	4.44%
Law/Corporate Library	31.58%	31.58%	10.53%	15.79%	10.53%
Government Agency/Department Library	28.57%	42.86%	28.57%	0.00%	0.00%

Table 4.63: Rate the usefulness of Wikipedia in your professional library work. Broken out by professional position at the library.

	HIGHLY USEFUL	USEFUL	OCCASIONALLY USEFUL	NOT VERY USEFUL	DO NOT USE/DON'T KNOW
Reference or Information Literacy	21.21%	39.39%	24.24%	6.06%	9.09%
Research or Subject Specialist	23.08%	30.77%	30.77%	15.38%	0.00%
Administration	20.93%	44.19%	23.26%	4.65%	6.98%
Technical Services or Cataloging	71.43%	28.57%	0.00%	0.00%	0.00%
Special Collections	20.00%	60.00%	0.00%	0.00%	20.00%
Acquisitions or Collection Development	66.67%	33.33%	0.00%	0.00%	0.00%

Table 4.64: Rate the usefulness of Wikipedia in your professional library work. Broken out by total library budget.

	HIGHLY USEFUL	USEFUL	OCCASIONALLY USEFUL	NOT VERY USEFUL	DO NOT USE/DON'T KNOW
Less than $1,000,000	31.58%	34.21%	15.79%	7.89%	10.53%
Between $1,000,000 - $5,000,000	18.92%	51.35%	24.32%	2.70%	2.70%
Between $5,000,000 - $10,000,000	12.50%	50.00%	12.50%	12.50%	12.50%
Over $10,000,000	31.82%	31.82%	27.27%	4.55%	4.55%

Table 4.65:   Rate the usefulness of Blogger.com in your professional library work.

	HIGHLY USEFUL	USEFUL	OCCASIONALLY USEFUL	NOT VERY USEFUL	DO NOT USE/DON'T KNOW
Entire Sample	7.77%	12.62%	14.56%	27.18%	37.86%

Table 4.66:   Rate the usefulness of Blogger.com in your professional library work. Broken out by type of library.

	HIGHLY USEFUL	USEFUL	OCCASIONALLY USEFUL	NOT VERY USEFUL	DO NOT USE/DON'T KNOW
Public Library	14.29%	14.29%	17.14%	11.43%	42.86%
College/University Library	7.14%	11.90%	14.29%	35.71%	30.95%
Law/Corporate Library	0.00%	5.26%	10.53%	36.84%	47.37%
Government Agency/Department Library	0.00%	28.57%	14.29%	28.57%	28.57%

Table 4.67:   Rate the usefulness of Blogger.com in your professional library work. Broken out by professional position at the library.

	HIGHLY USEFUL	USEFUL	OCCASIONALLY USEFUL	NOT VERY USEFUL	DO NOT USE/DON'T KNOW
Reference or Information Literacy	9.38%	15.63%	12.50%	25.00%	37.50%
Research or Subject Specialist	0.00%	15.38%	7.69%	53.85%	23.08%
Administration	11.36%	11.36%	11.36%	20.45%	45.45%
Technical Services or Cataloging	0.00%	14.29%	42.86%	14.29%	28.57%
Special Collections	0.00%	0.00%	0.00%	33.33%	66.67%
Acquisitions or Collection Development	0.00%	0.00%	66.67%	33.33%	0.00%

Table 4.68: Rate the usefulness of Blogger.com in your professional library work. Broken out by total library budget.

	HIGHLY USEFUL	USEFUL	OCCASIONALLY USEFUL	NOT VERY USEFUL	DO NOT USE/DON'T KNOW
Less than $1,000,000	5.41%	16.22%	10.81%	29.73%	37.84%
Between $1,000,000 - $5,000,000	11.11%	2.78%	22.22%	22.22%	41.67%
Between $5,000,000 - $10,000,000	0.00%	12.50%	12.50%	37.50%	37.50%
Over $10,000,000	9.09%	22.73%	9.09%	27.27%	31.82%

Table 4.69:   Rate the usefulness of Twitter in your professional library work.

	HIGHLY USEFUL	USEFUL	OCCASIONALLY USEFUL	NOT VERY USEFUL	DO NOT USE/DON'T KNOW
Entire Sample	12.26%	16.98%	18.87%	21.70%	30.19%

Table 4.70:   Rate the usefulness of Twitter in your professional library work. Broken out by type of library.

	HIGHLY USEFUL	USEFUL	OCCASIONALLY USEFUL	NOT VERY USEFUL	DO NOT USE/DON'T KNOW
Public Library	14.29%	25.71%	14.29%	14.29%	31.43%
College/University Library	8.89%	11.11%	22.22%	28.89%	28.89%
Law/Corporate Library	15.79%	10.53%	15.79%	26.32%	31.58%
Government Agency/Department Library	14.29%	28.57%	28.57%	0.00%	28.57%

Table 4.71:   Rate the usefulness of Twitter in your professional library work. Broken out by professional position at the library.

	HIGHLY USEFUL	USEFUL	OCCASIONALLY USEFUL	NOT VERY USEFUL	DO NOT USE/DON'T KNOW
Reference or Information Literacy	11.76%	14.71%	17.65%	20.59%	35.29%
Research or Subject Specialist	15.38%	15.38%	30.77%	23.08%	15.38%
Administration	11.36%	22.73%	20.45%	20.45%	25.00%
Technical Services or Cataloging	0.00%	14.29%	14.29%	0.00%	71.43%
Special Collections	0.00%	0.00%	0.00%	50.00%	50.00%
Acquisitions or Collection Development	66.67%	0.00%	0.00%	33.33%	0.00%

Table 4.72: Rate the usefulness of Twitter in your professional library work. Broken out by total library budget.

	HIGHLY USEFUL	USEFUL	OCCASIONALLY USEFUL	NOT VERY USEFUL	DO NOT USE/DON'T KNOW
Less than $1,000,000	8.11%	18.92%	16.22%	21.62%	35.14%
Between $1,000,000 - $5,000,000	15.79%	10.53%	15.79%	23.68%	34.21%
Between $5,000,000 - $10,000,000	12.50%	12.50%	25.00%	25.00%	25.00%
Over $10,000,000	13.04%	26.09%	26.09%	17.39%	17.39%

Table 4.73:   Rate the usefulness of Wordpress.com in your professional library work.

	HIGHLY USEFUL	USEFUL	OCCASIONALLY USEFUL	NOT VERY USEFUL	DO NOT USE/DON'T KNOW
Entire Sample	5.77%	18.27%	14.42%	24.04%	37.50%

Table 4.74:   Rate the usefulness of Wordpress.com in your professional library work. Broken out by type of library.

	HIGHLY USEFUL	USEFUL	OCCASIONALLY USEFUL	NOT VERY USEFUL	DO NOT USE/DON'T KNOW
Public Library	3.03%	21.21%	15.15%	18.18%	42.42%
College/University Library	11.11%	17.78%	17.78%	24.44%	28.89%
Law/Corporate Library	0.00%	10.53%	5.26%	26.32%	57.89%
Government Agency/Department Library	0.00%	28.57%	14.29%	42.86%	14.29%

Table 4.75:   Rate the usefulness of Wordpress.com in your professional library work. Broken out by professional position at the library.

	HIGHLY USEFUL	USEFUL	OCCASIONALLY USEFUL	NOT VERY USEFUL	DO NOT USE/DON'T KNOW
Reference or Information Literacy	8.82%	17.65%	14.71%	23.53%	35.29%
Research or Subject Specialist	0.00%	23.08%	15.38%	53.85%	7.69%
Administration	4.76%	16.67%	14.29%	16.67%	47.62%
Technical Services or Cataloging	0.00%	14.29%	28.57%	14.29%	42.86%
Special Collections	0.00%	25.00%	0.00%	25.00%	50.00%
Acquisitions or Collection Development	33.33%	33.33%	0.00%	33.33%	0.00%

Table 4.76: Rate the usefulness of Wordpress.com in your professional library work. Broken out by total library budget.

	HIGHLY USEFUL	USEFUL	OCCASIONALLY USEFUL	NOT VERY USEFUL	DO NOT USE/DON'T KNOW
Less than $1,000,000	8.11%	18.92%	10.81%	24.32%	37.84%
Between $1,000,000 - $5,000,000	0.00%	21.62%	18.92%	16.22%	43.24%
Between $5,000,000 - $10,000,000	0.00%	0.00%	12.50%	50.00%	37.50%
Over $10,000,000	13.64%	18.18%	13.64%	27.27%	27.27%

5. The Library and LibraryThing

Table 5.1: Which phrase best describes your understanding of and use of the internet site LibraryThing?

	DON'T REALLY KNOW WHAT IT IS	HAVE HEARD OF IT BUT WE DON'T USE IT	WE USE IT A LITTLE	WE USE IT A LOT	WE LOVE IT
Entire Sample	16.04%	61.32%	13.21%	4.72%	4.72%

Table 5.2: Which phrase best describes your understanding of and use of the internet site LibraryThing? Broken out by type of library.

	DON'T REALLY KNOW WHAT IT IS	HAVE HEARD OF IT BUT WE DON'T USE IT	WE USE IT A LITTLE	WE USE IT A LOT	WE LOVE IT
Public Library	5.71%	57.14%	20.00%	5.71%	11.43%
College/University Library	13.33%	71.11%	13.33%	2.22%	0.00%
Law/Corporate Library	47.37%	42.11%	0.00%	5.26%	5.26%
Government Agency/Department Library	0.00%	71.43%	14.29%	14.29%	0.00%

Table 5.3: Which phrase best describes your understanding of and use of the internet site LibraryThing? Broken out by professional position at the library.

	DON'T REALLY KNOW WHAT IT IS	HAVE HEARD OF IT BUT WE DON'T USE IT	WE USE IT A LITTLE	WE USE IT A LOT	WE LOVE IT
Reference or Information Literacy	8.82%	70.59%	14.71%	5.88%	0.00%
Research or Subject Specialist	7.69%	76.92%	7.69%	7.69%	0.00%
Administration	20.93%	51.16%	11.63%	4.65%	11.63%
Technical Services or Cataloging	28.57%	71.43%	0.00%	0.00%	0.00%
Special Collections	20.00%	80.00%	0.00%	0.00%	0.00%
Acquisitions or Collection Development	33.33%	0.00%	66.67%	0.00%	0.00%

Table 5.4:   Which phrase best describes your understanding of and use of the internet site LibraryThing? Broken out by total library budget.

	DON'T REALLY KNOW WHAT IT IS	HAVE HEARD OF IT BUT WE DON'T USE IT	WE USE IT A LITTLE	WE USE IT A LOT	WE LOVE IT
Less than $1,000,000	26.32%	52.63%	7.89%	5.26%	7.89%
Between $1,000,000 - $5,000,000	13.51%	64.86%	10.81%	5.41%	5.41%
Between $5,000,000 - $10,000,000	25.00%	75.00%	0.00%	0.00%	0.00%
Over $10,000,000	0.00%	65.22%	30.43%	4.35%	0.00%

If your library uses LibraryThing, briefly describe how you use it and how the library benefits:

1. We use it for organizing monthly book club process.

2. We are using it for our catalog. We direct all our patrons to it.

3. Learn about books, search titles. Overall use of website when needed, refer patrons to it all the time.

4. Will look for reviews and patterns in reading for patrons.

5. Think it is interesting and possibly useful for libraries but we do not use it.

6. It is used by our consortia to create tag clouds in the library catalog. It is a great service as patrons often find Library of Congress Subject Headings not intuitive and these tags are.

7. We love their recommendations feature and occasionally use it when we're stumped on authors or titles to recommend.

8. Post books on order in Library Thing http://www.mclib.info/book.html. Also link to tags.

9. Some branches have added their collections.

10. It is linked to our blog so that our counselors can borrow books.

11. Tagging is attached to our catalog.

12. We use both the free covers and the mobile LibraryAnywhere product.

13. Occasionally used for readers advisory.

14. We use it to promote our events. I use it to keep track of what I have read for Reader's Advisory. I once found a book a patron was looking for by asking on a romance reader's group.

15. We use it as a source for reader's advisory and as a holding place for staff created booklists.

16. I use it personally as a record of my reading, but the library does not use it.

17. I use LibraryThing personally as a kind of readers advisory, keeping track of what I have read (not necessarily what I own).

18. Good visual interface using widget imbed to website.

19. Did not see any benefits.

20. We have a VERY small book collection, so we add everything to LT as well as our local catalog; the most frequent use is to see who has considerable overlap with our collection, and then see what they have that we don't.

21. Used for readers advisory service, and particularly valuable for tagmash searches when patrons can't remember title or author.

22. I use it for book recommendations and occasionally for tracking down fiction books when the patron has spotty information.

6. The Library and Twitter

Table 6.1:   Does the library have a Twitter account?

	YES	NO
Entire Sample	40.57%	59.43%

Table 6.2:   Does the library have a Twitter account? Broken out by type of library.

	YES	NO
Public Library	61.76%	38.24%
College/University Library	41.30%	58.70%
Law/Corporate Library	5.26%	94.74%
Government Agency/Department Library	28.57%	71.43%

Table 6.3:   Does the library have a Twitter account? Broken out by professional position at the library.

	YES	NO
Reference or Information Literacy	42.42%	57.58%
Research or Subject Specialist	30.77%	69.23%
Administration	38.64%	61.36%
Technical Services or Cataloging	42.86%	57.14%
Special Collections	60.00%	40.00%
Acquisitions or Collection Development	33.33%	66.67%

Table 6.4:   Does the library have a Twitter account? Broken out by total library budget.

	YES	NO
Less than $1,000,000	23.68%	76.32%
Between $1,000,000 - $5,000,000	39.47%	60.53%
Between $5,000,000 - $10,000,000	50.00%	50.00%
Over $10,000,000	68.18%	31.82%

Table 6.5: How many tweets does your library send out in a typical or average month?

	MEAN	MEDIAN	MINIMUM	MAXIMUM
Entire Sample	32.17	16.00	0.00	300.00

Table 6.6: How many tweets does your library send out in a typical or average month? Broken out by type of library.

	MEAN	MEDIAN	MINIMUM	MAXIMUM
Public Library	46.45	22.50	0.00	300.00
College/University Library	19.17	5.50	0.00	150.00
Law/Corporate Library	0.00	0.00	0.00	0.00
Government Agency/Department Library	22.50	22.50	20.00	25.00

Table 6.7: How many tweets does your library send out in a typical or average month? Broken out by professional position at the library.

	MEAN	MEDIAN	MINIMUM	MAXIMUM
Reference or Information Literacy	21.79	15.00	0.00	63.00
Research or Subject Specialist	13.25	13.00	2.00	25.00
Administration	40.16	15.00	0.00	300.00
Technical Services or Cataloging	16.00	16.00	2.00	30.00
Special Collections	16.00	16.00	16.00	16.00
Acquisitions or Collection Development	150.00	150.00	150.00	150.00

Table 6.8: How many tweets does your library send out in a typical or average month? Broken out by total library budget.

	MEAN	MEDIAN	MINIMUM	MAXIMUM
Less than $1,000,000	8.44	5.00	0.00	25.00
Between $1,000,000 - $5,000,000	46.73	10.00	0.00	300.00
Between $5,000,000 - $10,000,000	7.00	5.00	0.00	18.00
Over $10,000,000	39.54	27.00	2.00	150.00

Table 6.9: To the best of your knowledge how many subscribers does your library's Twitter account have?

	MEAN	MEDIAN	MINIMUM	MAXIMUM
Entire Sample	416.67	144.50	0.00	2,500.00

Table 6.10: To the best of your knowledge how many subscribers does your library's Twitter account have? Broken out by type of library.

	MEAN	MEDIAN	MINIMUM	MAXIMUM
Public Library	568.82	185.00	0.00	2500.00
College/University Library	232.50	93.00	0.00	1000.00
Law/Corporate Library	0.00	0.00	0.00	0.00
Government Agency/Department Library	805.00	805.00	647.00	963.00

Table 6.11: To the best of your knowledge how many subscribers does your library's Twitter account have? Broken out by professional position at the library.

	MEAN	MEDIAN	MINIMUM	MAXIMUM
Reference or Information Literacy	535.18	291.00	0.00	2500.00
Research or Subject Specialist	434.00	373.50	26.00	963.00
Administration	356.38	93.00	0.00	1768.00
Technical Services or Cataloging	253.00	253.00	6.00	500.00
Special Collections	139.00	139.00	139.00	139.00
Acquisitions or Collection Development	1000.00	1000.00	1000.00	1000.00

Table 6.12:   To the best of your knowledge how many subscribers does your library's Twitter account have? Broken out by total library budget.

	MEAN	MEDIAN	MINIMUM	MAXIMUM
Less than $1,000,000	255.88	107.50	0.00	963.00
Between $1,000,000 - $5,000,000	262.33	65.50	0.00	1768.00
Between $5,000,000 - $10,000,000	483.33	150.00	0.00	1300.00
Over $10,000,000	642.69	300.00	26.00	2500.00

7. Social Networking Sites

Table 7.1: Rate the usefulness of MySpace to your work or the library in general.

	VERY USEFUL	USEFUL	SOMEWHAT USEFUL	NOT VERY USEFUL
Entire Sample	0.00%	0.95%	12.38%	86.67%

Table 7.2: Rate the usefulness of MySpace to your work or the library in general. Broken out by type of library.

	VERY USEFUL	USEFUL	SOMEWHAT USEFUL	NOT VERY USEFUL
Public Library	0.00%	0.00%	11.76%	88.24%
College/University Library	0.00%	2.22%	17.78%	80.00%
Law/Corporate Library	0.00%	0.00%	5.26%	94.74%
Government Agency/Department Library	0.00%	0.00%	0.00%	100.00%

Table 7.3: Rate the usefulness of MySpace to your work or the library in general. Broken out by professional position at the library.

	VERY USEFUL	USEFUL	SOMEWHAT USEFUL	NOT VERY USEFUL
Reference or Information Literacy	0.00%	3.13%	9.38%	87.50%
Research or Subject Specialist	0.00%	0.00%	0.00%	100.00%
Administration	0.00%	0.00%	18.18%	81.82%
Technical Services or Cataloging	0.00%	0.00%	0.00%	100.00%
Special Collections	0.00%	0.00%	0.00%	100.00%
Acquisitions or Collection Development	0.00%	0.00%	33.33%	66.67%

Table 7.4: **Rate the usefulness of MySpace to your work or the library in general. Broken out by total library budget.**

	VERY USEFUL	USEFUL	SOMEWHAT USEFUL	NOT VERY USEFUL
Less than $1,000,000	0.00%	2.63%	10.53%	86.84%
Between $1,000,000 - $5,000,000	0.00%	0.00%	15.79%	84.21%
Between $5,000,000 - $10,000,000	0.00%	0.00%	25.00%	75.00%
Over $10,000,000	0.00%	0.00%	4.76%	95.24%

Table 7.5: Rate the usefulness of Facebook to your work or the library in general.

	VERY USEFUL	USEFUL	SOMEWHAT USEFUL	NOT VERY USEFUL
Entire Sample	21.70%	33.02%	24.53%	20.75%

Table 7.6: Rate the usefulness of Facebook to your work or the library in general. Broken out by type of library.

	VERY USEFUL	USEFUL	SOMEWHAT USEFUL	NOT VERY USEFUL
Public Library	44.12%	38.24%	8.82%	8.82%
College/University Library	15.22%	34.78%	28.26%	21.74%
Law/Corporate Library	0.00%	26.32%	31.58%	42.11%
Government Agency/Department Library	14.29%	14.29%	57.14%	14.29%

Table 7.7: Rate the usefulness of Facebook to your work or the library in general. Broken out by professional position at the library.

	VERY USEFUL	USEFUL	SOMEWHAT USEFUL	NOT VERY USEFUL
Reference or Information Literacy	15.15%	45.45%	18.18%	21.21%
Research or Subject Specialist	0.00%	7.69%	76.92%	15.38%
Administration	36.36%	27.27%	15.91%	20.45%
Technical Services or Cataloging	14.29%	42.86%	0.00%	42.86%
Special Collections	20.00%	40.00%	20.00%	20.00%
Acquisitions or Collection Development	0.00%	66.67%	33.33%	0.00%

Table 7.8: Rate the usefulness of Facebook to your work or the library in general. Broken out by total library budget.

	VERY USEFUL	USEFUL	SOMEWHAT USEFUL	NOT VERY USEFUL
Less than $1,000,000	23.68%	21.05%	28.95%	26.32%
Between $1,000,000 - $5,000,000	21.05%	39.47%	15.79%	23.68%
Between $5,000,000 - $10,000,000	12.50%	50.00%	25.00%	12.50%
Over $10,000,000	22.73%	36.36%	31.82%	9.09%

Table 7.9: Rate the usefulness of Bebo to your work or the library in general.

	VERY USEFUL	USEFUL	SOMEWHAT USEFUL	NOT VERY USEFUL
Entire Sample	0.00%	0.99%	0.99%	98.02%

Table 7.10: Rate the usefulness of Bebo to your work or the library in general. Broken out by type of library.

	VERY USEFUL	USEFUL	SOMEWHAT USEFUL	NOT VERY USEFUL
Public Library	0.00%	0.00%	3.23%	96.77%
College/University Library	0.00%	2.27%	0.00%	97.73%
Law/Corporate Library	0.00%	0.00%	0.00%	100.00%
Government Agency/Department Library	0.00%	0.00%	0.00%	100.00%

Table 7.11: Rate the usefulness of Bebo to your work or the library in general. Broken out by professional position at the library.

	VERY USEFUL	USEFUL	SOMEWHAT USEFUL	NOT VERY USEFUL
Reference or Information Literacy	0.00%	3.23%	3.23%	93.55%
Research or Subject Specialist	0.00%	0.00%	0.00%	100.00%
Administration	0.00%	0.00%	0.00%	100.00%
Technical Services or Cataloging	0.00%	0.00%	0.00%	100.00%
Special Collections	0.00%	0.00%	0.00%	100.00%
Acquisitions or Collection Development	0.00%	0.00%	0.00%	100.00%

Table 7.12: Rate the usefulness of Bebo to your work or the library in general. Broken out by total library budget.

	VERY USEFUL	USEFUL	SOMEWHAT USEFUL	NOT VERY USEFUL
Less than $1,000,000	0.00%	0.00%	0.00%	100.00%
Between $1,000,000 - $5,000,000	0.00%	2.70%	0.00%	97.30%
Between $5,000,000 - $10,000,000	0.00%	0.00%	0.00%	100.00%
Over $10,000,000	0.00%	0.00%	5.26%	94.74%

Table 7.13: Rate the usefulness of Friendster to your work or the library in general.

	VERY USEFUL	USEFUL	SOMEWHAT USEFUL	NOT VERY USEFUL
Entire Sample	0.00%	0.00%	1.00%	99.00%

Table 7.14: Rate the usefulness of Friendster to your work or the library in general. Broken out by type of library.

	VERY USEFUL	USEFUL	SOMEWHAT USEFUL	NOT VERY USEFUL
Public Library	0.00%	0.00%	0.00%	100.00%
College/University Library	0.00%	0.00%	2.27%	97.73%
Law/Corporate Library	0.00%	0.00%	0.00%	100.00%
Government Agency/Department Library	0.00%	0.00%	0.00%	100.00%

Table 7.15: Rate the usefulness of Friendster to your work or the library in general. Broken out by professional position at the library.

	VERY USEFUL	USEFUL	SOMEWHAT USEFUL	NOT VERY USEFUL
Reference or Information Literacy	0.00%	0.00%	3.23%	96.77%
Research or Subject Specialist	0.00%	0.00%	0.00%	100.00%
Administration	0.00%	0.00%	0.00%	100.00%
Technical Services or Cataloging	0.00%	0.00%	0.00%	100.00%
Special Collections	0.00%	0.00%	0.00%	100.00%
Acquisitions or Collection Development	0.00%	0.00%	0.00%	100.00%

Table 7.16: Rate the usefulness of Friendster to your work or the library in general. Broken out by total library budget.

	VERY USEFUL	USEFUL	SOMEWHAT USEFUL	NOT VERY USEFUL
Less than $1,000,000	0.00%	0.00%	0.00%	100.00%
Between $1,000,000 - $5,000,000	0.00%	0.00%	2.78%	97.22%
Between $5,000,000 - $10,000,000	0.00%	0.00%	0.00%	100.00%
Over $10,000,000	0.00%	0.00%	0.00%	100.00%

Table 7.17:   Rate the usefulness of Ning to your work or the library in general.

	VERY USEFUL	USEFUL	SOMEWHAT USEFUL	NOT VERY USEFUL
Entire Sample	0.00%	3.03%	3.03%	93.94%

Table 7.18:   Rate the usefulness of Ning to your work or the library in general. Broken out by type of library.

	VERY USEFUL	USEFUL	SOMEWHAT USEFUL	NOT VERY USEFUL
Public Library	0.00%	3.23%	6.45%	90.32%
College/University Library	0.00%	0.00%	0.00%	100.00%
Law/Corporate Library	0.00%	11.11%	0.00%	88.89%
Government Agency/Department Library	0.00%	0.00%	14.29%	85.71%

Table 7.19:   Rate the usefulness of Ning to your work or the library in general. Broken out by professional position at the library.

	VERY USEFUL	USEFUL	SOMEWHAT USEFUL	NOT VERY USEFUL
Reference or Information Literacy	0.00%	3.33%	3.33%	93.33%
Research or Subject Specialist	0.00%	0.00%	7.69%	92.31%
Administration	0.00%	5.00%	2.50%	92.50%
Technical Services or Cataloging	0.00%	0.00%	0.00%	100.00%
Special Collections	0.00%	0.00%	0.00%	100.00%
Acquisitions or Collection Development	0.00%	0.00%	0.00%	100.00%

Table 7.20: Rate the usefulness of Ning to your work or the library in general. Broken out by total library budget.

	VERY USEFUL	USEFUL	SOMEWHAT USEFUL	NOT VERY USEFUL
Less than $1,000,000	0.00%	2.70%	2.70%	94.59%
Between $1,000,000 - $5,000,000	0.00%	0.00%	5.56%	94.44%
Between $5,000,000 - $10,000,000	0.00%	14.29%	0.00%	85.71%
Over $10,000,000	0.00%	5.26%	0.00%	94.74%

Table 7.21: Rate the usefulness of Hi5 to your work or the library in general.

	VERY USEFUL	USEFUL	SOMEWHAT USEFUL	NOT VERY USEFUL
Entire Sample	0.00%	0.00%	0.00%	100.00%

Table 7.22: Rate the usefulness of Orkut to your work or the library in general.

	VERY USEFUL	USEFUL	SOMEWHAT USEFUL	NOT VERY USEFUL
Entire Sample	0.00%	0.00%	0.00%	100.00%

Table 7.23: Rate the usefulness of MyLife to your work or the library in general.

	VERY USEFUL	USEFUL	SOMEWHAT USEFUL	NOT VERY USEFUL
Entire Sample	0.00%	0.00%	1.00%	99.00%

Table 7.24: Rate the usefulness of MyLife to your work or the library in general. Broken out by type of library.

	VERY USEFUL	USEFUL	SOMEWHAT USEFUL	NOT VERY USEFUL
Public Library	0.00%	0.00%	0.00%	100.00%
College/University Library	0.00%	0.00%	2.27%	97.73%
Law/Corporate Library	0.00%	0.00%	0.00%	100.00%
Government Agency/Department Library	0.00%	0.00%	0.00%	100.00%

Table 7.25: Rate the usefulness of MyLife to your work or the library in general. Broken out by professional position at the library.

	VERY USEFUL	USEFUL	SOMEWHAT USEFUL	NOT VERY USEFUL
Reference or Information Literacy	0.00%	0.00%	0.00%	100.00%
Research or Subject Specialist	0.00%	0.00%	0.00%	100.00%
Administration	0.00%	0.00%	2.50%	97.50%
Technical Services or Cataloging	0.00%	0.00%	0.00%	100.00%
Special Collections	0.00%	0.00%	0.00%	100.00%
Acquisitions or Collection Development	0.00%	0.00%	0.00%	100.00%

Table 7.26: Rate the usefulness of MyLife to your work or the library in general. Broken out by total library budget.

	VERY USEFUL	USEFUL	SOMEWHAT USEFUL	NOT VERY USEFUL
Less than $1,000,000	0.00%	0.00%	2.70%	97.30%
Between $1,000,000 - $5,000,000	0.00%	0.00%	0.00%	100.00%
Between $5,000,000 - $10,000,000	0.00%	0.00%	0.00%	100.00%
Over $10,000,000	0.00%	0.00%	0.00%	100.00%

Table 7.27:   Rate the usefulness of Multiply to your work or the library in general.

	VERY USEFUL	USEFUL	SOMEWHAT USEFUL	NOT VERY USEFUL
Entire Sample	0.00%	1.01%	0.00%	98.99%

Table 7.28:   Rate the usefulness of Multiply to your work or the library in general. Broken out by type of library.

	VERY USEFUL	USEFUL	SOMEWHAT USEFUL	NOT VERY USEFUL
Public Library	0.00%	0.00%	0.00%	100.00%
College/University Library	0.00%	2.33%	0.00%	97.67%
Law/Corporate Library	0.00%	0.00%	0.00%	100.00%
Government Agency/Department Library	0.00%	0.00%	0.00%	100.00%

Table 7.29:   Rate the usefulness of Multiply to your work or the library in general. Broken out by professional position at the library.

	VERY USEFUL	USEFUL	SOMEWHAT USEFUL	NOT VERY USEFUL
Reference or Information Literacy	0.00%	3.33%	0.00%	96.67%
Research or Subject Specialist	0.00%	0.00%	0.00%	100.00%
Administration	0.00%	0.00%	0.00%	100.00%
Technical Services or Cataloging	0.00%	0.00%	0.00%	100.00%
Special Collections	0.00%	0.00%	0.00%	100.00%
Acquisitions or Collection Development	0.00%	0.00%	0.00%	100.00%

Table 7.30: Rate the usefulness of Multiply to your work or the library in general. Broken out by total library budget.

	VERY USEFUL	USEFUL	SOMEWHAT USEFUL	NOT VERY USEFUL
Less than $1,000,000	0.00%	0.00%	0.00%	100.00%
Between $1,000,000 - $5,000,000	0.00%	2.78%	0.00%	97.22%
Between $5,000,000 - $10,000,000	0.00%	0.00%	0.00%	100.00%
Over $10,000,000	0.00%	0.00%	0.00%	100.00%

Table 7.31: If it has a presence on the site, approximately how many unique visits does the library receive per month on average to MySpace?

	MEAN	MEDIAN	MINIMUM	MAXIMUM
Entire Sample	0.00	0.00	0.00	0.00

Table 7.32: If it has a presence on the site, approximately how many unique visits does the library receive per month on average to Facebook?

	MEAN	MEDIAN	MINIMUM	MAXIMUM
Entire Sample	971.66	100.00	3.00	12,000.00

Table 7.33: If it has a presence on the site, approximately how many unique visits does the library receive per month on average to Facebook? Broken out by type of library.

	MEAN	MEDIAN	MINIMUM	MAXIMUM
Public Library	1,214.37	200.00	6.00	12,000.00
College/University Library	637.73	60.00	3.00	5,800.00
Law/Corporate Library	5.00	5.00	5.00	5.00
Government Agency/Department Library	1,000.00	1,000.00	1,000.00	1,000.00

Table 7.34: If it has a presence on the site, approximately how many unique visits does the library receive per month on average to Facebook? Broken out by total library budget.

	MEAN	MEDIAN	MINIMUM	MAXIMUM
Less than $1,000,000	693.80	80.00	5.00	5,247.00
Between $1,000,000 - $5,000,000	94.83	42.50	0.00	712.00
Between $5,000,000 - $10,000,000	4,400.00	1,000.00	200.00	12,000.00
Over $10,000,000	1,321.14	526.00	12.00	5,800.00

Table 7.35: If it has a presence on other social networking sites, approximately how many unique visits does the library receive per month on average to these sites?

	MEAN	MEDIAN	MINIMUM	MAXIMUM
Entire Sample	5,710.00	400.00	40.00	22,000.00

Table 7.36:   Has your library developed specific pages on Facebook or on other social networks for specific collections or library departments?

	YES	NO
Entire Sample	35.29%	64.71%

Table 7.37:   Has your library developed specific pages on Facebook or on other social networks for specific collections or library departments? Broken out by type of library.

	YES	NO
Public Library	39.39%	60.61%
College/University Library	44.44%	55.56%
Law/Corporate Library	11.76%	88.24%
Government Agency/Department Library	14.29%	85.71%

Table 7.38:   Has your library developed specific pages on Facebook or on other social networks for specific collections or library departments? Broken out by professional position at the library.

	YES	NO
Reference or Information Literacy	39.39%	60.61%
Research or Subject Specialist	25.00%	75.00%
Administration	29.27%	70.73%
Technical Services or Cataloging	42.86%	57.14%
Special Collections	60.00%	40.00%
Acquisitions or Collection Development	33.33%	66.67%

Table 7.39:   Has your library developed specific pages on Facebook or on other social networks for specific collections or library departments? Broken out by total library budget.

	YES	NO
Less than $1,000,000	18.42%	81.58%
Between $1,000,000 - $5,000,000	40.00%	60.00%
Between $5,000,000 - $10,000,000	25.00%	75.00%
Over $10,000,000	61.90%	38.10%

8. Use of Amazon

Table 8.1: Has the library ever purchased an e-book from Amazon or an e-book in conjunction with a print title?

	YES	NO
Entire Sample	35.71%	64.29%

Table 8.2: Has the library ever purchased an e-book from Amazon or an e-book in conjunction with a print title? Broken out by type of library.

	YES	NO
Public Library	19.35%	80.65%
College/University Library	52.38%	47.62%
Law/Corporate Library	36.84%	63.16%
Government Agency/Department Library	0.00%	100.00%

Table 8.3: Has the library ever purchased an e-book from Amazon or an e-book in conjunction with a print title? Broken out by professional position at the library.

	YES	NO
Reference or Information Literacy	44.83%	55.17%
Research or Subject Specialist	41.67%	58.33%
Administration	26.83%	73.17%
Technical Services or Cataloging	42.86%	57.14%
Special Collections	40.00%	60.00%
Acquisitions or Collection Development	33.33%	66.67%

Table 8.4: Has the library ever purchased an e-book from Amazon or an e-book in conjunction with a print title? Broken out by total library budget.

	YES	NO
Less than $1,000,000	25.00%	75.00%
Between $1,000,000 - $5,000,000	27.03%	72.97%
Between $5,000,000 - $10,000,000	40.00%	60.00%
Over $10,000,000	70.00%	30.00%

Table 8.5: How much has the library spent on Amazon in the past year to acquire traditional books, e-books or parts of books?

	MEAN	MEDIAN	MINIMUM	MAXIMUM
Entire Sample	$6,823.40	$500.00	$0.00	$150,000.00

Table 8.6: How much has the library spent on Amazon in the past year to acquire traditional books, e-books or parts of books? Broken out by type of library.

	MEAN	MEDIAN	MINIMUM	MAXIMUM
Public Library	$2,144.20	$500.00	$0.00	$10,000.00
College/University Library	$15,491.18	$1,000.00	$0.00	$150,000.00
Law/Corporate Library	$756.67	$600.00	$40.00	$2,500.00
Government Agency/Department Library	$1,066.67	$1,200.00	$0.00	$2,000.00

Table 8.7: How much has the library spent on Amazon in the past year to acquire traditional books, e-books or parts of books? Broken out by professional position at the library.

	MEAN	MEDIAN	MINIMUM	MAXIMUM
Reference or Information Literacy	$3,443.75	$1,275.00	$0.00	$10,000.00
Research or Subject Specialist	$5,566.67	$1,200.00	$0.00	$25,000.00
Administration	$2,652.30	$500.00	$0.00	$35,000.00
Technical Services or Cataloging	$300.00	$300.00	$100.00	$500.00
Special Collections	$500.00	$0.00	$0.00	$1,500.00
Acquisitions or Collection Development	$76,500.00	$76,500.00	$3,000.00	$150,000.00

Table 8.8:   How much has the library spent on Amazon in the past year
to acquire traditional books, e-books or parts of books? Broken out by total
library budget.

	MEAN	MEDIAN	MINIMUM	MAXIMUM
Less than $1,000,000	$2,888.12	$500.00	$0.00	$35,000.00
Between $1,000,000 - $5,000,000	$3,523.33	$500.00	$0.00	$30,000.00
Between $5,000,000 - $10,000,000	$2,000.00	$2,000.00	$2,000.00	$2,000.00
Over $10,000,000	$45,000.00	$15,000.00	$0.00	$150,000.00

Table 8.9: How much has the library spent on all other online booksellers in the past year to acquire traditional books, e-books or parts of books?

	MEAN	MEDIAN	MINIMUM	MAXIMUM
Entire Sample	15224.97	5000.00	0.00	100000.00

Table 8.10: How much has the library spent on all other online booksellers in the past year to acquire traditional books, e-books or parts of books? Broken out by type of library.

	MEAN	MEDIAN	MINIMUM	MAXIMUM
Public Library	$16,075.00	$850.00	$0.00	$100,000.00
College/University Library	$19,808.33	$6,500.00	$200.00	$100,000.00
Law/Corporate Library	$4,874.80	$5,000.00	$74.00	$10,000.00
Government Agency/Department Library	$8,500.00	$8,500.00	$5,000.00	$12,000.00

Table 8.11: How much has the library spent on all other online booksellers in the past year to acquire traditional books, e-books or parts of books? Broken out by professional position at the library.

	MEAN	MEDIAN	MINIMUM	MAXIMUM
Reference or Information Literacy	$15,222.22	$5,000.00	$0.00	$100,000.00
Research or Subject Specialist	$38,000.00	$9,000.00	$5,000.00	$100,000.00
Administration	$11,021.08	$700.00	$0.00	$75,000.00
Technical Services or Cataloging	$18,733.33	$6,000.00	$200.00	$50,000.00
Special Collections	$20,000.00	$20,000.00	$20,000.00	$20,000.00
Acquisitions or Collection Development	$1,000.00	$1,000.00	$1,000.00	$1,000.00

Table 8.12:   How much has the library spent on all other online booksellers in the past year to acquire traditional books, e-books or parts of books? Broken out by total library budget.

	MEAN	MEDIAN	MINIMUM	MAXIMUM
Less than $1,000,000	$16,279.63	$5,000.00	$0.00	$100,000.00
Between $1,000,000 - $5,000,000	$9,254.55	$5,000.00	$0.00	$50,000.00
Between $5,000,000 - $10,000,000	$700.00	$700.00	$700.00	$700.00
Over $10,000,000	$36,333.33	$9,000.00	$0.00	$100,000.00

Table 8.13: Does the library in any way take advantage of the Amazon web services program that allows libraries to use cover images, reviews, book descriptions and other book-related information from the Amazon site in the library OPAC or in other library contexts?

	YES, QUITE EXTENSIVELY	YES, SOMEWHAT	NO, AND WE HAVE NO PLANS TO	NO, BUT WE HAVE PLANS TO	NO, AND WE HAVE NEVER HEARD OF THIS PROGRAM
Entire Sample	8.42%	22.11%	37.89%	12.63%	18.95%

Table 8.14: Does the library in any way take advantage of the Amazon web services program that allows libraries to use cover images, reviews, book descriptions and other book-related information from the Amazon site in the library OPAC or in other library contexts? Broken out by type of library.

	YES, QUITE EXTENSIVELY	YES, SOME-WHAT	NO, AND WE HAVE NO PLANS TO	NO, BUT WE HAVE PLANS TO	NO, AND WE HAVE NEVER HEARD OF THIS PROGRAM
Public Library	13.33%	20.00%	50.00%	3.33%	13.33%
College/University Library	10.00%	37.50%	30.00%	10.00%	12.50%
Law/Corporate Library	0.00%	0.00%	26.32%	31.58%	42.11%
Government Agency/Department Library	0.00%	0.00%	66.67%	16.67%	16.67%

Table 8.15:   Does the library in any way take advantage of the Amazon web services program that allows libraries to use cover images, reviews, book descriptions and other book-related information from the Amazon site in the library OPAC or in other library contexts? Broken out by professional position at the library.

	YES, QUITE EXTENSIVELY	YES, SOME-WHAT	NO, AND WE HAVE NO PLANS TO	NO, BUT WE HAVE PLANS TO	NO, AND WE HAVE NEVER HEARD OF THIS PROGRAM
Reference or Information Literacy	14.29%	32.14%	39.29%	3.57%	10.71%
Research or Subject Specialist	9.09%	0.00%	45.45%	27.27%	18.18%
Administration	7.50%	17.50%	40.00%	12.50%	22.50%
Technical Services or Cataloging	0.00%	14.29%	14.29%	28.57%	42.86%
Special Collections	0.00%	40.00%	40.00%	0.00%	20.00%
Acquisitions or Collection Development	0.00%	33.33%	33.33%	33.33%	0.00%

Table 8.16:   Does the library in any way take advantage of the Amazon web services program that allows libraries to use cover images, reviews, book descriptions and other book-related information from the Amazon site in the library OPAC or in other library contexts? Broken out by total library budget.

	YES, QUITE EXTENSIVELY	YES, SOME-WHAT	NO, AND WE HAVE NO PLANS TO	NO, BUT WE HAVE PLANS TO	NO, AND WE HAVE NEVER HEARD OF THIS PROGRAM
Less than $1,000,000	0.00%	22.22%	33.33%	25.00%	19.44%
Between $1,000,000 - $5,000,000	16.67%	27.78%	30.56%	8.33%	16.67%
Between $5,000,000 - $10,000,000	0.00%	0.00%	40.00%	0.00%	60.00%
Over $10,000,000	11.11%	16.67%	61.11%	0.00%	11.11%

9. Video & Photo Sharing

Table 9.1:   Does the library have one or more YouTube accounts?

	YES	NO	NO, BUT WE PLAN TO SIGN UP WITHIN THE NEXT YEAR
Entire Sample	36.63%	57.43%	5.94%

Table 9.2:   Does the library have one or more YouTube accounts? Broken out by type of library.

	YES	NO	NO, BUT WE PLAN TO SIGN UP WITHIN THE NEXT YEAR
Public Library	51.52%	39.39%	9.09%
College/University Library	42.22%	53.33%	4.44%
Law/Corporate Library	5.56%	94.44%	0.00%
Government Agency/Department Library	0.00%	80.00%	20.00%

Table 9.3:   Does the library have one or more YouTube accounts? Broken out by professional position at the library.

	YES	NO	NO, BUT WE PLAN TO SIGN UP WITHIN THE NEXT YEAR
Reference or Information Literacy	46.88%	46.88%	6.25%
Research or Subject Specialist	18.18%	81.82%	0.00%
Administration	28.57%	61.90%	9.52%
Technical Services or Cataloging	42.86%	57.14%	0.00%
Special Collections	60.00%	40.00%	0.00%
Acquisitions or Collection Development	66.67%	33.33%	0.00%

Table 9.4: Does the library have one or more YouTube accounts? Broken out by total library budget.

	YES	NO	NO, BUT WE PLAN TO SIGN UP WITHIN THE NEXT YEAR
Less than $1,000,000	13.89%	80.56%	5.56%
Between $1,000,000 - $5,000,000	40.54%	59.46%	0.00%
Between $5,000,000 - $10,000,000	33.33%	50.00%	16.67%
Over $10,000,000	68.18%	18.18%	13.64%

Table 9.5: Do you use AOL Video in your professional library work?

	YES	NO
Entire Sample	1.02%	98.98%

Table 9.6: Do you use AOL Video in your professional library work? Broken out by type of library.

	YES	NO
Public Library	3.13%	96.88%
College/University Library	0.00%	100.00%
Law/Corporate Library	0.00%	100.00%
Government Agency/Department Library	0.00%	100.00%

Table 9.7: Do you use AOL Video in your professional library work? Broken out by professional position at the library.

	YES	NO
Reference or Information Literacy	0.00%	100.00%
Research or Subject Specialist	0.00%	100.00%
Administration	2.38%	97.62%
Technical Services or Cataloging	0.00%	100.00%
Special Collections	0.00%	100.00%
Acquisitions or Collection Development	0.00%	100.00%

Table 9.8: Do you use AOL Video in your professional library work? Broken out by total library budget.

	YES	NO
Less than $1,000,000	0.00%	100.00%
Between $1,000,000 - $5,000,000	2.86%	97.14%
Between $5,000,000 - $10,000,000	0.00%	100.00%
Over $10,000,000	0.00%	100.00%

Table 9.9:   Do you use Blip TV in your professional library work?

	YES	NO
Entire Sample	4.12%	95.88%

Table 9.10:   Do you use Blip TV in your professional library work? Broken out by type of library.

	YES	NO
Public Library	12.50%	87.50%
College/University Library	0.00%	100.00%
Law/Corporate Library	0.00%	100.00%
Government Agency/Department Library	0.00%	100.00%

Table 9.11:   Do you use Blip TV in your professional library work? Broken out by professional position at the library.

	YES	NO
Reference or Information Literacy	3.45%	96.55%
Research or Subject Specialist	0.00%	100.00%
Administration	7.14%	92.86%
Technical Services or Cataloging	0.00%	100.00%
Special Collections	0.00%	100.00%
Acquisitions or Collection Development	0.00%	100.00%

Table 9.12:   Do you use Blip TV in your professional library work? Broken out by total library budget.

	YES	NO
Less than $1,000,000	2.86%	97.14%
Between $1,000,000 - $5,000,000	2.86%	97.14%
Between $5,000,000 - $10,000,000	0.00%	100.00%
Over $10,000,000	10.00%	90.00%

Table 9.13:   Do you use Brightcove in your professional library work?

	YES	NO
Entire Sample	1.04%	98.96%

Table 9.14:   Do you use Brightcove in your professional library work? Broken out by type of library.

	YES	NO
Public Library	0.00%	100.00%
College/University Library	0.00%	100.00%
Law/Corporate Library	5.56%	94.44%
Government Agency/Department Library	0.00%	100.00%

Table 9.15:   Do you use Brightcove in your professional library work? Broken out by professional position at the library.

	YES	NO
Reference or Information Literacy	0.00%	100.00%
Research or Subject Specialist	0.00%	100.00%
Administration	0.00%	100.00%
Technical Services or Cataloging	0.00%	100.00%
Special Collections	0.00%	100.00%
Acquisitions or Collection Development	33.33%	66.67%

Table 9.16:   Do you use Brightcove in your professional library work? Broken out by total library budget.

	YES	NO
Less than $1,000,000	2.94%	97.06%
Between $1,000,000 - $5,000,000	0.00%	100.00%
Between $5,000,000 - $10,000,000	0.00%	100.00%
Over $10,000,000	0.00%	100.00%

Table 9.17:   Do you use DailyMotion in your professional library work?

	YES	NO
Entire Sample	1.05%	98.95%

Table 9.18:   Do you use DailyMotion in your professional library work? Broken out by type of library.

	YES	NO
Public Library	3.13%	96.88%
College/University Library	0.00%	100.00%
Law/Corporate Library	0.00%	100.00%
Government Agency/Department Library	0.00%	100.00%

Table 9.19:   Do you use DailyMotion in your professional library work? Broken out by professional position at the library.

	YES	NO
Reference or Information Literacy	0.00%	100.00%
Research or Subject Specialist	0.00%	100.00%
Administration	0.00%	100.00%
Technical Services or Cataloging	0.00%	100.00%
Special Collections	0.00%	100.00%
Acquisitions or Collection Development	33.33%	66.67%

Table 9.20:   Do you use DailyMotion in your professional library work? Broken out by total library budget.

	YES	NO
Less than $1,000,000	0.00%	100.00%
Between $1,000,000 - $5,000,000	2.86%	97.14%
Between $5,000,000 - $10,000,000	0.00%	100.00%
Over $10,000,000	0.00%	100.00%

Table 9.21: Do you use Facebook in your professional library work?

	YES	NO
Entire Sample	73.00%	27.00%

Table 9.22: Do you use Facebook in your professional library work? Broken out by type of library.

	YES	NO
Public Library	81.82%	18.18%
College/University Library	76.74%	23.26%
Law/Corporate Library	47.37%	52.63%
Government Agency/Department Library	80.00%	20.00%

Table 9.23: Do you use Facebook in your professional library work? Broken out by professional position at the library.

	YES	NO
Reference or Information Literacy	73.33%	26.67%
Research or Subject Specialist	72.73%	27.27%
Administration	72.09%	27.91%
Technical Services or Cataloging	71.43%	28.57%
Special Collections	80.00%	20.00%
Acquisitions or Collection Development	66.67%	33.33%

Table 9.24: Do you use Facebook in your professional library work? Broken out by total library budget.

	YES	NO
Less than $1,000,000	60.00%	40.00%
Between $1,000,000 - $5,000,000	80.56%	19.44%
Between $5,000,000 - $10,000,000	85.71%	14.29%
Over $10,000,000	77.27%	22.73%

Table 9.25:   Do you use Flickr Video in your professional library work?

	YES	NO
Entire Sample	18.56%	81.44%

Table 9.26:   Do you use Flickr Video in your professional library work? Broken out by type of library.

	YES	NO
Public Library	21.88%	78.13%
College/University Library	21.43%	78.57%
Law/Corporate Library	5.56%	94.44%
Government Agency/Department Library	20.00%	80.00%

Table 9.27:   Do you use Flickr Video in your professional library work? Broken out by professional position at the library.

	YES	NO
Reference or Information Literacy	20.69%	79.31%
Research or Subject Specialist	0.00%	100.00%
Administration	21.43%	78.57%
Technical Services or Cataloging	14.29%	85.71%
Special Collections	0.00%	100.00%
Acquisitions or Collection Development	33.33%	66.67%

Table 9.28:   Do you use Flickr Video in your professional library work? Broken out by total library budget.

	YES	NO
Less than $1,000,000	20.59%	79.41%
Between $1,000,000 - $5,000,000	20.00%	80.00%
Between $5,000,000 - $10,000,000	14.29%	85.71%
Over $10,000,000	14.29%	85.71%

Table 9.29: Do you use GoFish in your professional library work?

	YES	NO
Entire Sample	6.06%	93.94%

Table 9.30: Do you use GoFish in your professional library work? Broken out by type of library.

	YES	NO
Public Library	3.13%	96.88%
College/University Library	11.63%	88.37%
Law/Corporate Library	0.00%	100.00%
Government Agency/Department Library	0.00%	100.00%

Table 9.31: Do you use GoFish in your professional library work? Broken out by professional position at the library.

	YES	NO
Reference or Information Literacy	6.67%	93.33%
Research or Subject Specialist	0.00%	100.00%
Administration	7.14%	92.86%
Technical Services or Cataloging	0.00%	100.00%
Special Collections	20.00%	80.00%
Acquisitions or Collection Development	0.00%	100.00%

Table 9.32: Do you use GoFish in your professional library work? Broken out by total library budget.

	YES	NO
Less than $1,000,000	8.33%	91.67%
Between $1,000,000 - $5,000,000	5.71%	94.29%
Between $5,000,000 - $10,000,000	0.00%	100.00%
Over $10,000,000	4.76%	95.24%

Table 9.33: Do you use Google Buzz in your professional library work?

	YES	NO
Entire Sample	4.08%	95.92%

Table 9.34: Do you use Google Buzz in your professional library work? Broken out by type of library.

	YES	NO
Public Library	3.13%	96.88%
College/University Library	2.38%	97.62%
Law/Corporate Library	10.53%	89.47%
Government Agency/Department Library	0.00%	100.00%

Table 9.35: Do you use Google Buzz in your professional library work? Broken out by professional position at the library.

	YES	NO
Reference or Information Literacy	3.45%	96.55%
Research or Subject Specialist	18.18%	81.82%
Administration	2.38%	97.62%
Technical Services or Cataloging	0.00%	100.00%
Special Collections	0.00%	100.00%
Acquisitions or Collection Development	0.00%	100.00%

Table 9.36: Do you use Google Buzz in your professional library work? Broken out by total library budget.

	YES	NO
Less than $1,000,000	2.86%	97.14%
Between $1,000,000 - $5,000,000	5.71%	94.29%
Between $5,000,000 - $10,000,000	0.00%	100.00%
Over $10,000,000	4.76%	95.24%

Table 9.37:   Do you use Google Video in your professional library work?

	YES	NO
Entire Sample	17.00%	83.00%

Table 9.38:   Do you use Google Video in your professional library work? Broken out by type of library.

	YES	NO
Public Library	12.50%	87.50%
College/University Library	22.73%	77.27%
Law/Corporate Library	15.79%	84.21%
Government Agency/Department Library	0.00%	100.00%

Table 9.39:   Do you use Google Video in your professional library work? Broken out by professional position at the library.

	YES	NO
Reference or Information Literacy	22.58%	77.42%
Research or Subject Specialist	27.27%	72.73%
Administration	11.90%	88.10%
Technical Services or Cataloging	0.00%	100.00%
Special Collections	20.00%	80.00%
Acquisitions or Collection Development	33.33%	66.67%

Table 9.40:   Do you use Google Video in your professional library work? Broken out by total library budget.

	YES	NO
Less than $1,000,000	16.67%	83.33%
Between $1,000,000 - $5,000,000	17.14%	82.86%
Between $5,000,000 - $10,000,000	0.00%	100.00%
Over $10,000,000	22.73%	77.27%

Table 9.41:   Do you use Hulu in your professional library work?

	YES	NO
Entire Sample	17.53%	82.47%

Table 9.42:   Do you use Hulu in your professional library work? Broken out by type of library.

	YES	NO
Public Library	9.68%	90.32%
College/University Library	19.05%	80.95%
Law/Corporate Library	31.58%	68.42%
Government Agency/Department Library	0.00%	100.00%

Table 9.43:   Do you use Hulu in your professional library work? Broken out by professional position at the library.

	YES	NO
Reference or Information Literacy	13.79%	86.21%
Research or Subject Specialist	27.27%	72.73%
Administration	14.63%	85.37%
Technical Services or Cataloging	14.29%	85.71%
Special Collections	0.00%	100.00%
Acquisitions or Collection Development	66.67%	33.33%

Table 9.44:   Do you use Hulu in your professional library work? Broken out by total library budget.

	YES	NO
Less than $1,000,000	14.29%	85.71%
Between $1,000,000 - $5,000,000	22.86%	77.14%
Between $5,000,000 - $10,000,000	33.33%	66.67%
Over $10,000,000	9.52%	90.48%

Table 9.45:   Do you use MetaCafe in your professional library work?

	YES	NO
Entire Sample	2.08%	97.92%

Table 9.46:   Do you use MetaCafe in your professional library work? Broken out by type of library.

	YES	NO
Public Library	3.23%	96.77%
College/University Library	2.38%	97.62%
Law/Corporate Library	0.00%	100.00%
Government Agency/Department Library	0.00%	100.00%

Table 9.47:   Do you use MetaCafe in your professional library work? Broken out by professional position at the library.

	YES	NO
Reference or Information Literacy	0.00%	100.00%
Research or Subject Specialist	0.00%	100.00%
Administration	4.88%	95.12%
Technical Services or Cataloging	0.00%	100.00%
Special Collections	0.00%	100.00%
Acquisitions or Collection Development	0.00%	100.00%

Table 9.48:   Do you use MetaCafe in your professional library work? Broken out by total library budget.

	YES	NO
Less than $1,000,000	2.94%	97.06%
Between $1,000,000 - $5,000,000	2.86%	97.14%
Between $5,000,000 - $10,000,000	0.00%	100.00%
Over $10,000,000	0.00%	100.00%

Table 9.49: **Do you use Photobucket in your professional library work?**

	YES	NO
Entire Sample	11.11%	88.89%

Table 9.50: **Do you use Photobucket in your professional library work? Broken out by type of library.**

	YES	NO
Public Library	21.21%	78.79%
College/University Library	4.76%	95.24%
Law/Corporate Library	5.26%	94.74%
Government Agency/Department Library	20.00%	80.00%

Table 9.51: **Do you use Photobucket in your professional library work? Broken out by professional position at the library.**

	YES	NO
Reference or Information Literacy	6.90%	93.10%
Research or Subject Specialist	0.00%	100.00%
Administration	16.28%	83.72%
Technical Services or Cataloging	0.00%	100.00%
Special Collections	0.00%	100.00%
Acquisitions or Collection Development	66.67%	33.33%

Table 9.52: **Do you use Photobucket in your professional library work? Broken out by total library budget.**

	YES	NO
Less than $1,000,000	11.43%	88.57%
Between $1,000,000 - $5,000,000	13.89%	86.11%
Between $5,000,000 - $10,000,000	0.00%	100.00%
Over $10,000,000	9.52%	90.48%

Table 9.53:   Do you use Revver in your professional library work?

	YES	NO
Entire Sample	0.00%	100.00%

Table 9.54:   Do you use Viddler in your professional library work?

	YES	NO
Entire Sample	0.00%	100.00%

Table 9.55:   Do you use Vimeo in your professional library work?

	YES	NO
Entire Sample	12.37%	87.63%

Table 9.56:   Do you use Vimeo in your professional library work? Broken out by type of library.

	YES	NO
Public Library	16.13%	83.87%
College/University Library	7.14%	92.86%
Law/Corporate Library	21.05%	78.95%
Government Agency/Department Library	0.00%	100.00%

Table 9.57:   Do you use Vimeo in your professional library work? Broken out by professional position at the library.

	YES	NO
Reference or Information Literacy	7.14%	92.86%
Research or Subject Specialist	18.18%	81.82%
Administration	9.52%	90.48%
Technical Services or Cataloging	28.57%	71.43%
Special Collections	0.00%	100.00%
Acquisitions or Collection Development	66.67%	33.33%

Table 9.58: Do you use Vimeo in your professional library work? Broken out by total library budget.

	YES	NO
Less than $1,000,000	5.71%	94.29%
Between $1,000,000 - $5,000,000	17.14%	82.86%
Between $5,000,000 - $10,000,000	14.29%	85.71%
Over $10,000,000	15.00%	85.00%

Table 9.59:   Do you use Vzaar in your professional library work?

	YES	NO
Entire Sample	1.04%	98.96%

Table 9.60:   Do you use Vzaar in your professional library work? Broken out by type of library.

	YES	NO
Public Library	3.13%	96.88%
College/University Library	0.00%	100.00%
Law/Corporate Library	0.00%	100.00%
Government Agency/Department Library	0.00%	100.00%

Table 9.61:   Do you use Vzaar in your professional library work? Broken out by professional position at the library.

	YES	NO
Reference or Information Literacy	3.70%	96.30%
Research or Subject Specialist	0.00%	100.00%
Administration	0.00%	100.00%
Technical Services or Cataloging	0.00%	100.00%
Special Collections	0.00%	100.00%
Acquisitions or Collection Development	0.00%	100.00%

Table 9.62:   Do you use Vzaar in your professional library work? Broken out by total library budget.

	YES	NO
Less than $1,000,000	0.00%	100.00%
Between $1,000,000 - $5,000,000	0.00%	100.00%
Between $5,000,000 - $10,000,000	0.00%	100.00%
Over $10,000,000	4.76%	95.24%

Table 9.63:   Do you use Yahoo Video in your professional library work?

	YES	NO
Entire Sample	7.22%	92.78%

Table 9.64:   Do you use Yahoo Video in your professional library work? Broken out by type of library.

	YES	NO
Public Library	3.23%	96.77%
College/University Library	7.14%	92.86%
Law/Corporate Library	15.79%	84.21%
Government Agency/Department Library	0.00%	100.00%

Table 9.65:   Do you use Yahoo Video in your professional library work? Broken out by professional position at the library.

	YES	NO
Reference or Information Literacy	3.45%	96.55%
Research or Subject Specialist	9.09%	90.91%
Administration	4.88%	95.12%
Technical Services or Cataloging	0.00%	100.00%
Special Collections	20.00%	80.00%
Acquisitions or Collection Development	33.33%	66.67%

Table 9.66:   Do you use Yahoo Video in your professional library work? Broken out by total library budget.

	YES	NO
Less than $1,000,000	2.86%	97.14%
Between $1,000,000 - $5,000,000	14.29%	85.71%
Between $5,000,000 - $10,000,000	0.00%	100.00%
Over $10,000,000	5.00%	95.00%

Table 9.67:   Do you use Yfrog in your professional library work?

	YES	NO
Entire Sample	3.06%	96.94%

Table 9.68:   Do you use Yfrog in your professional library work? Broken out by type of library.

	YES	NO
Public Library	3.03%	96.97%
College/University Library	4.76%	95.24%
Law/Corporate Library	0.00%	100.00%
Government Agency/Department Library	0.00%	100.00%

Table 9.69:   Do you use Yfrog in your professional library work? Broken out by professional position at the library.

	YES	NO
Reference or Information Literacy	3.57%	96.43%
Research or Subject Specialist	0.00%	100.00%
Administration	2.33%	97.67%
Technical Services or Cataloging	14.29%	85.71%
Special Collections	0.00%	100.00%
Acquisitions or Collection Development	0.00%	100.00%

Table 9.70:   Do you use Yfrog in your professional library work? Broken out by total library budget.

	YES	NO
Less than $1,000,000	0.00%	100.00%
Between $1,000,000 - $5,000,000	5.56%	94.44%
Between $5,000,000 - $10,000,000	0.00%	100.00%
Over $10,000,000	4.76%	95.24%

Table 9.71:   Do you use YouTube in your professional library work?

	YES	NO
Entire Sample	63.27%	36.73%

Table 9.72:   Do you use YouTube in your professional library work? Broken out by type of library.

	YES	NO
Public Library	63.64%	36.36%
College/University Library	78.57%	21.43%
Law/Corporate Library	31.58%	68.42%
Government Agency/Department Library	50.00%	50.00%

Table 9.73:   Do you use YouTube in your professional library work? Broken out by professional position at the library.

	YES	NO
Reference or Information Literacy	76.67%	23.33%
Research or Subject Specialist	63.64%	36.36%
Administration	48.84%	51.16%
Technical Services or Cataloging	71.43%	28.57%
Special Collections	80.00%	20.00%
Acquisitions or Collection Development	100.00%	0.00%

Table 9.74:   Do you use YouTube in your professional library work? Broken out by total library budget.

	YES	NO
Less than $1,000,000	45.71%	54.29%
Between $1,000,000 - $5,000,000	57.14%	42.86%
Between $5,000,000 - $10,000,000	100.00%	0.00%
Over $10,000,000	90.48%	9.52%

Table 9.75:   How many visits did the library get to its YouTube site in the past year?

	MEAN	MEDIAN	MINIMUM	MAXIMUM
Entire Sample	3,833.71	245.00	0.00	30,800.00

Table 9.76:   How many visits did the library get to its YouTube site in the past year? Broken out by type of library.

	MEAN	MEDIAN	MINIMUM	MAXIMUM
Public Library	3,620.43	1,000.00	35.00	10,000.00
College/University Library	4,597.08	147.50	0.00	30,800.00
Law/Corporate Library	0.00	0.00	0.00	0.00
Government Agency/Department Library	0.00	0.00	0.00	0.00

Table 9.77:   How many visits did the library get to its YouTube site in the past year? Broken out by total library budget.

	MEAN	MEDIAN	MINIMUM	MAXIMUM
Less than $1,000,000	86.25	50.00	0.00	245.00
Between $1,000,000 - $5,000,000	888.00	20.00	0.00	5,000.00
Between $5,000,000 - $10,000,000	35.00	35.00	35.00	35.00
Over $10,000,000	8,212.44	5,000.00	0.00	30,800.00

Table 9.78:   Has the library ever posted any photos of the library or library special events on Flickr (the Yahoo photo sharing site)?

	YES	NO
Entire Sample	34.58%	65.42%

Table 9.79: Has the library ever posted any photos of the library or library special events on Flickr (the Yahoo photo sharing site)? Broken out by type of library.

	YES	NO
Public Library	54.29%	45.71%
College/University Library	34.78%	65.22%
Law/Corporate Library	5.26%	94.74%
Government Agency/Department Library	14.29%	85.71%

Table 9.80: Has the library ever posted any photos of the library or library special events on Flickr (the Yahoo photo sharing site)? Broken out by professional position at the library.

	YES	NO
Reference or Information Literacy	50.00%	50.00%
Research or Subject Specialist	7.69%	92.31%
Administration	31.82%	68.18%
Technical Services or Cataloging	42.86%	57.14%
Special Collections	20.00%	80.00%
Acquisitions or Collection Development	33.33%	66.67%

Table 9.81: Has the library ever posted any photos of the library or library special events on Flickr (the Yahoo photo sharing site)? Broken out by total library budget.

	YES	NO
Less than $1,000,000	23.68%	76.32%
Between $1,000,000 - $5,000,000	34.21%	65.79%
Between $5,000,000 - $10,000,000	25.00%	75.00%
Over $10,000,000	56.52%	43.48%

Table 9.82:   Has the library ever posted any photos from the library collection on Flickr?

	YES	NO
Entire Sample	13.08%	86.92%

Table 9.83:   Has the library ever posted any photos from the library collection on Flickr? Broken out by type of library.

	YES	NO
Public Library	14.29%	85.71%
College/University Library	17.39%	82.61%
Law/Corporate Library	5.26%	94.74%
Government Agency/Department Library	0.00%	100.00%

Table 9.84:   Has the library ever posted any photos from the library collection on Flickr? Broken out by professional position at the library.

	YES	NO
Reference or Information Literacy	14.71%	85.29%
Research or Subject Specialist	7.69%	92.31%
Administration	9.09%	90.91%
Technical Services or Cataloging	14.29%	85.71%
Special Collections	20.00%	80.00%
Acquisitions or Collection Development	33.33%	66.67%

Table 9.85:   Has the library ever posted any photos from the library collection on Flickr? Broken out by total library budget.

	YES	NO
Less than $1,000,000	10.53%	89.47%
Between $1,000,000 - $5,000,000	13.16%	86.84%
Between $5,000,000 - $10,000,000	0.00%	100.00%
Over $10,000,000	21.74%	78.26%

Table 9.86: Has the library ever posted any photos taken by library patrons on Flickr?

	YES	NO
Entire Sample	6.98%	93.02%

Table 9.87: Has the library ever posted any photos taken by library patrons on Flickr? Broken out by type of library.

	YES	NO
Public Library	8.82%	91.18%
College/University Library	9.38%	90.63%
Law/Corporate Library	0.00%	100.00%
Government Agency/Department Library	0.00%	100.00%

Table 9.88: Has the library ever posted any photos taken by library patrons on Flickr? Broken out by professional position at the library.

	YES	NO
Reference or Information Literacy	7.41%	92.59%
Research or Subject Specialist	11.11%	88.89%
Administration	5.41%	94.59%
Technical Services or Cataloging	16.67%	83.33%
Special Collections	0.00%	100.00%
Acquisitions or Collection Development	0.00%	100.00%

Table 9.89: Has the library ever posted any photos taken by library patrons on Flickr? Broken out by total library budget.

	YES	NO
Less than $1,000,000	3.23%	96.77%
Between $1,000,000 - $5,000,000	0.00%	100.00%
Between $5,000,000 - $10,000,000	0.00%	100.00%
Over $10,000,000	27.78%	72.22%

Table 9.90: Has the library ever used YouTube in training library patrons to use the library?

	YES	NO
Entire Sample	21.50%	78.50%

Table 9.91: Has the library ever used YouTube in training library patrons to use the library? Broken out by type of library.

	YES	NO
Public Library	17.14%	82.86%
College/University Library	34.78%	65.22%
Law/Corporate Library	5.26%	94.74%
Government Agency/Department Library	0.00%	100.00%

Table 9.92: Has the library ever used YouTube in training library patrons to use the library? Broken out by professional position at the library.

	YES	NO
Reference or Information Literacy	29.41%	70.59%
Research or Subject Specialist	7.69%	92.31%
Administration	18.18%	81.82%
Technical Services or Cataloging	42.86%	57.14%
Special Collections	20.00%	80.00%
Acquisitions or Collection Development	0.00%	100.00%

Table 9.93: Has the library ever used YouTube in training library patrons to use the library? Broken out by total library budget.

	YES	NO
Less than $1,000,000	10.53%	89.47%
Between $1,000,000 - $5,000,000	15.79%	84.21%
Between $5,000,000 - $10,000,000	37.50%	62.50%
Over $10,000,000	43.48%	56.52%

If the library has posted videos or photos about itself or its collections on internet photo and video sites, please mention a few of the most useful or prominent sites.

1. Google_scholar onu_passwords

2. A few times

3. Library Snapshot Day, Training video

4. Flickr - YouTube - Facebook - Twitter - Foursquare - LinkedIn - Blogger - Yelp

5. YouTube--for fundraising

6. Flickr, Facebook, YouTube

7. facebook.com

8. We've posted a few training videos on YouTube, but that's it. They're not heavily used, and have gone out of date.

9. Flickr

10. We post our photos and videos on our own web site server.

11. We post videos and pictures on our Facebook page.

12. YouTube and Flickr

13. Flickr

14. FamilySearch.org

15. Vimeo

16. Can't remember

17. Has a digital collection on our library and consortium websites.

18. Facebook

19. Content DM

20. University of Wisconsin Digital Collections

21. YouTube

22. YouTube and Flickr

23. Primal scream; cookie break; zombie library; christmas baskets; renovations

24. YouTube, Flickr

10. The Library and Google Books

Table 10.1: Which phrase best describes your library staff's use of Google Books?

	WE DON'T REALLY USE IT	WE USE IT OCCASIONALLY	WE USE IT EXTENSIVELY
Entire Sample	38.38%	56.57%	5.05%

Table 10.2: Which phrase best describes your library staff's use of Google Books? Broken out by type of library.

	WE DON'T REALLY USE IT	WE USE IT OCCASIONALLY	WE USE IT EXTENSIVELY
Public Library	62.50%	37.50%	0.00%
College/University Library	20.93%	72.09%	6.98%
Law/Corporate Library	31.58%	63.16%	5.26%
Government Agency/Department Library	60.00%	20.00%	20.00%

Table 10.3: Which phrase best describes your library staff's use of Google Books? Broken out by professional position at the library.

	WE DON'T REALLY USE IT	WE USE IT OCCASIONALLY	WE USE IT EXTENSIVELY
Reference or Information Literacy	35.48%	61.29%	3.23%
Research or Subject Specialist	9.09%	63.64%	27.27%
Administration	51.22%	48.78%	0.00%
Technical Services or Cataloging	57.14%	42.86%	0.00%
Special Collections	0.00%	100.00%	0.00%
Acquisitions or Collection Development	33.33%	33.33%	33.33%

Table 10.4: Which phrase best describes your library staff's use of Google Books? Broken out by total library budget.

	WE DON'T REALLY USE IT	WE USE IT OCCASIONALLY	WE USE IT EXTENSIVELY
Less than $1,000,000	41.67%	55.56%	2.78%
Between $1,000,000 - $5,000,000	43.24%	51.35%	5.41%
Between $5,000,000 - $10,000,000	16.67%	83.33%	0.00%
Over $10,000,000	30.00%	60.00%	10.00%

Table 10.5: Which phrase best captures the library's plans for contributing content to Google Books?

	WE HAVE ALREADY DIGITIZED PART OF OUR COLLECTION AND CONTRIBUTE SOME OF OUR NON-COPYRIGHT WORKS TO GOOGLE BOOKS	WE HAVE ALREADY DIGITIZED PARTS OF OUR COLLECTION BUT HAVE NOT CONTRIBUTED TO GOOGLE BOOKS	WE HAVE NOT DIGITIZED ANY PART OF OUR COLLECTION BUT PLAN TO IN THE NEAR FUTURE	WE HAVE NOT DIGITIZED ANY PART OF OUR COLLECTION AND DO NOT PLAN TO IN THE NEAR FUTURE
Entire Sample	6.12%	16.33%	3.06%	74.49%

Table 10.6: Which phrase best captures the library's plans for contributing content to Google Books? Broken out by type of library.

	WE HAVE ALREADY DIGITIZED PART OF OUR COLLECTION AND CONTRIBUTE SOME OF OUR NON-COPYRIGHT WORKS TO GOOGLE BOOKS	WE HAVE ALREADY DIGITIZED PARTS OF OUR COLLECTION BUT HAVE NOT CONTRIBUTED TO GOOGLE BOOKS	WE HAVE NOT DIGITIZED ANY PART OF OUR COLLECTION BUT PLAN TO IN THE NEAR FUTURE	WE HAVE NOT DIGITIZED ANY PART OF OUR COLLECTION AND DO NOT PLAN TO IN THE NEAR FUTURE
Public Library	3.23%	6.45%	0.00%	90.32%
College/University Library	11.63%	27.91%	6.98%	53.49%
Law/Corporate Library	0.00%	5.26%	0.00%	94.74%
Government Agency/Department Library	0.00%	20.00%	0.00%	80.00%

Table 10.7: Which phrase best captures the library's plans for contributing content to Google Books? Broken out by professional position at the library.

	WE HAVE ALREADY DIGITIZED PART OF OUR COLLECTION AND CONTRIBUTE SOME OF OUR NON-COPYRIGHT WORKS TO GOOGLE BOOKS	WE HAVE ALREADY DIGITIZED PARTS OF OUR COLLECTION BUT HAVE NOT CONTRIBUTED TO GOOGLE BOOKS	WE HAVE NOT DIGITIZED ANY PART OF OUR COLLECTION BUT PLAN TO IN THE NEAR FUTURE	WE HAVE NOT DIGITIZED ANY PART OF OUR COLLECTION AND DO NOT PLAN TO IN THE NEAR FUTURE
Reference or Information Literacy	13.33%	16.67%	3.33%	66.67%
Research or Subject Specialist	18.18%	27.27%	0.00%	54.55%
Administration	0.00%	7.32%	2.44%	90.24%
Technical Services or Cataloging	0.00%	28.57%	0.00%	71.43%
Special Collections	0.00%	40.00%	20.00%	40.00%
Acquisitions or Collection Development	0.00%	0.00%	0.00%	100.00%

Table 10.8: Which phrase best captures the library's plans for contributing content to Google Books? Broken out by total library budget.

	WE HAVE ALREADY DIGITIZED PART OF OUR COLLECTION AND CONTRIBUTE SOME OF OUR NON-COPYRIGHT WORKS TO GOOGLE BOOKS	WE HAVE ALREADY DIGITIZED PART OF OUR COLLECTION BUT HAVE NOT CONTRIBUTED TO GOOGLE BOOKS	WE HAVE NOT DIGITZED ANY PART OF OUR COLLECTION BUT PLAN TO IN THE NEAR FUTURE	WE HAVE NOT DIGITIZED ANY PART OF OUR COLLECTION AND DO NOT PLAN TO IN THE NEAR FUTURE
Less than $1,000,000	0.00%	11.11%	5.56%	83.33%
Between $1,000,000 - $5,000,000	2.70%	16.22%	2.70%	78.38%
Between $5,000,000 - $10,000,000	0.00%	16.67%	0.00%	83.33%
Over $10,000,000	26.32%	26.32%	0.00%	47.37%